Links Lore

Links Lore

Dramatic Moments and Forgotten Milestones from Golf's History

Peter F. Stevens

Brassey's

WASHINGTON • LONDON

First Brassey's paperback edition 2000

Editorial Offices:
22883 Quicksilver Drive
Dulles, VA 20166

Order Department:
P.O. Box 960
Herndon, VA 20172

Brassey's books are available at special discounts for bulk purchases for sales promotions, premiums, fund-raising, or educational use.

Library of Congress Cataloging-in-Publication Data

Stevens, Peter F.
    Links lore : dramatic moments and forgotten milestones from golf's history / Peter F. Stevens.
        p.   cm.
    Includes bibliographical references (p.) and index.
    ISBN 1-57488-265-1
    1. Golf—History. I. Title
GV963.S74   1998
796.352′09--dc21   98-8638
                                                                  CIP

Designed by Pen & Palette Unlimited

Front dustjacket photographs courtesy of the U.S. Golf Association

10 9 8 7 6 5 4 3 2 1

Printed in Canada

Contents

List of Illustrations ix

Preface x

1. Cabin Fever

Snow Man 1

Southbound 4

Inside Moves 6

2. What's in a Name?

Wild Bill 9

The *Real* Tony Manero 10

The Other Palmer 13

Jack and the Giant 15

3. The Law and the Links

Kolf, Anyone? 24

Until Death Do Us Part 26

Accidents Happen 27

On Strike 29

The Road to Ruin 31

Never on a Sunday 32

Grand Theft Golf 36
The Boys Are Back 38
The Caddie's Revenge 39
John Q. Public 41

4. A Place in the Sun
The Eye of the Storm 43
A Card-Carrying Member 48
A Family Affair 52
East Meets West 55
Fighting Two Battles 57
"I'll See You in Court" 59
Zero Handicap 68
A Snowball's Chance 72
"All We Need Is the Chance" 81

5. A Better Mousetrap
Fit to a Tee 88
Bauxite Brassies 91
The Man of Steel 93
Four for the Price of One 98
The Weed-Whacker 99
Putting on Blinders 100
Positive Reinforcement 101
Let There Be Light 102
A Puff of Smoke 103
The Eyes Have It 104
Man and Machine 106
Atomic Golf 107
All the Right Moves 108

6. Helping the Hapless
The Father of American Golf? 110
Loopers 113

Knock Hell Out of It! 115
Golfology 117

7. **Who Needs Lessons?**
One-Shot Wonder 119
Swing from the Heels 120
Diegeling 122
Same Cup, Same Game 124

8. **Grip It and Rip It**
Far and Sure 126
Of Ruthian Proportions 129

9. **Misery Loves Company**
Reversal of Fortune 132
Ill Winds 134
Read 'Em and Weep 136

10. **Join the Club**
The Apple Tree Gang 138
Gaiters and Guffaws 139
Bottoms Up! 140
No Peeking 141
Ladies' Day 142
The One and Only 143

11. **"You've Come a Long Way"**
The Mother of American Golf 146
Blasted Hopes 149
Mrs. Brown's Crown 153
A Star Is Born 157
Beyond Our Shores 162
No Greater Honor 166
The "Bewitching Blonde" 167

12. In Print and Pictures

Here to Stay 173

Worth a Thousand Words 174

An Animated Round 175

13. Look Out Below!

Bombs Away! 177

The Flying Wedge 178

From Fairway to Airway 181

14. A Hothead and a Hula Dancer

The Profane Pro 185

No Hula Allowed 187

15. "Show Me the Money"

Connecting the Dots 188

Whitewash 190

Cardboard Cash 191

Dough for the Doughboys 191

Sand Dollars 195

A Born Saleswoman 199

16. It's Never Too Late

The Wright Stuff? 202

An Ageless Wonder 203

Sources 207

Index 209

List of Illustrations

William "Wild Bill" Melhorn 10
Tony Manero 12
Jack Fleck 22
John Shippen 47
Al Espinosa 53
Bill Spiller 64
Ed Furgol 71
Charlie Sifford 85
George F. Grant's turn-of-the-century patent for
    first golf tee 89
1908 advertisement for state-of-the-art golf clubs 92
William Davis's four-sided putter, 1904 98
James Ross Brown's rake-iron, 1905 100
Jim Reynolds tests General Electric's 1932 swing
    speed measuring device 105
1950s swing aid 107
"Loopers"at St. Andrew's Golf Club, 1888 114
Bobby Jones 116
Chip Hilton 121
Leo Diegel 123
Willie Park, Jr. 127
Babe Ruth 129
Jackie Pung 136
Morris County Golf Club founders, 1893 151
Mrs. Charles S. Brown 154
Beatrix Hoyt 161
Peg Curtis 164
Edith Cummings 169
Bobby Cruickshank 180
Johnny Bulla 183
Spalding's 1906 "Dot" golf ball advertisement 189
1907 advertisement for ball paint 190
Jock Hutchison 194
Gene Sarazen 198
Helen Hicks 200

Preface

While working on an article for *Golf Magazine* a couple of years ago, I interviewed attorney Archie Reid, who told me that his great-great-great grandfather John Reid, "the Father of American Golf," played against his wife in America's first mixed foursome in 1889, lost to her and her partner, John Upham, and refused to play another round with or against her again. When I repeated the anecdote to a golfer and editor whose knowledge of the game's history was formidable, he admitted that he had never heard it. What about *The New York Times*'s 1922 eulogy for Reid's better half, Lizzie Reid, as "the Mother of American Golf"? I asked. My editor had not heard of this either, and suggested that I might want to "write something" about the Reids' milestone mixed foursome.

With the suggestion in mind, I began sifting through hundreds of golfing tidbits I had come across in old newspapers and magazines and transcripts of interviews conducted for my articles in *Golf Journal, Golf Magazine,* and a wide range of other publications. Some of these pieces of golf's past were compelling, some humorous, and some curious. Each, I felt, said something unique about how golf in America got from there to here, "there" stretching back to the 1600s, long before John Reid and his buddies put club to ball in a Yonkers, New York, cow pasture in 1888.

Yet when I shared these anecdotes, I discovered that many bona fide golf history buffs were not aware of them—and quite a few friends and editors suggested that they should be gathered in one place. That place is *Links Lore.*

In researching and writing this book, I have enlisted the help and the advice of numerous people. I want to thank Rich Skyzinski, the managing editor at *Golf Journal.* Rich's reverence for the game's true past and his commitment to it shine in every issue of the magazine. The same holds true for Brett Avery, *Golf Journal*'s editor in chief.

I also want to thank *Golf Magazine*'s Tara Gravel and Mike Purkey, both of whom are outstanding editors and writers. Their enthusiasm for obscure stories of golf's past helped point me to *Links Lore.*

Every author should have the chance to work with an editor such as Don McKeon, at Brassey's. I have had the great good fortune to reap his insight and his editorial expertise twice.

I also want to thank Linda Ridinger Smith, production director at Brassey's, for her hard work and her patience on my behalf.

To my agent Frank Weimann, of the Literary Group International, I am grateful for his advice and his expertise.

To Maxine Vigliotta, of the USGA Golf House Photo Archives, my special thanks for all of her help not only with this book, but also with my articles over the past few years. I do not know how she copes with the volume of requests she receives, but she always comes through. The same is true of Saundra Sheffer.

I would also like to express my gratitude to *The Iowan Magazine*'s editor, Jay Wagner, a friend, avid golfer, terrific editor, and supporter of this project.

Anyone who wants to know anything about antique clubs, balls, and "everything golf" should look up Leo J. Kelly, Jr., proprietor of the Old Chicago Golf Shop. I am glad I did.

To John Turnbull, head professional at the Scotch Plains, New Jersey, Golf Club, I am indebted for all of the material he shared about John Shippen and the Shady Grove Golf Club. Henry Nichols, head professional at Shinnecock Hills, provided great material about the club's early days and its vibrant cast of turn-of-the-century characters.

As always, Mary Clark and Linda Beeler, of the Thomas Crane Public Library, in Quincy, Massachusetts, fielded all my requests for obscure books and magazines and somehow got them into my hands.

Ted Kiegiel, head professional at the Carolina Country Club, PGA Class-A instructor, fellow writer, and friend, has given me an even deeper appreciation of the game.

Last but certainly not least, my thanks, as always, to Peg, Paula, Karen, and Greg Stevens—Greg was the first in the family bitten by the golf bug. My thanks also for the encouragement from Joe Axelrod, Val Doran, Theresa and Mike Bidwell, and Patricia, Jim, John, Milt, Joanna, Pat, Atsumi Marsh, and David Pearlman, family and friends all.

1

Cabin Fever

Snow Man

On a road in Dummerston, Vermont, in the winter of 1893, passersby gaped at their newest neighbor. The bespectacled man trudged across his snow-shrouded eleven acres with his mashie (five-iron), brassie (two-wood), and spoon (three-wood) and sprayed red gutta-percha balls at, around, and into tin cans scattered across his pasture. Wrapped in a bulky woolen coat, he flailed away, each swing kicking up a spray of white.

The USGA would soon proclaim the "madman" in the meadow the creator of "snow golf." His name? Rudyard Kipling.

When the twenty-eight-year-old Kipling, his American-born wife, Carrie, and their infant daughter moved into their rural Vermont digs in the summer of 1893, he sought privacy and inspiration for his muse on enough real estate for one of his other passions: golf. The much-traveled Englishman dubbed his rambling slope-roofed wooden manse Naulakha, which means "jewel beyond price" in the Hindi tongue. All across his acreage he hammered up "No Trespassing" signs, and inside his spacious study he shoved tall bookcases against the Tiffany stained-glass windows to thwart "peepers" eager for a glimpse of the increasingly popular author. He wrote *The Jungle Books* and *Captains Courageou*s in that secluded study and began a third classic, the *Just So Stories.*

On Naulakha's pastureland, Kipling showed far less concern about peepers. Anyone riding or strolling most afternoons along the road could stop and stare at the diminutive writer. After mornings spent filling sheafs of paper, he would cap his bottle of India ink, put down his pen, grab his kit of clubs, scurry outdoors and into the meadow, and unleash golf strokes as erratic as his prose was smooth. Gawkers discovered that with his poor eyesight and his lack of coordination, Kipling played the game with more enthusiasm than skill. On several occasions, locals spotted guest Sir Arthur Conan Doyle, the creator of Sherlock Holmes, striding across that meadow with his mustachioed, golf-mad crony.

To the surprise of his New England neighbors, Kipling found a fellow lover of the links in the local Episcopalian church's pastor, the Reverend C. O. Day. The preacher took no offense that the writer rarely attended his golf buddy's Sunday sermons, and the twosome regularly met in the pasture to work on their strokes.

What did the cleric's flock *really* think about the starry Englishman who seemingly cared less about keeping the Sabbath than about cracking gutta-perchies across his estate? One could say that many locals found him eccentric. The *Burlington News* related: "Neighbors say he is strange, never carries money; wears shabby clothes; drives shaggy horses; plays with his baby." When paying bills in Dummerston or in nearby Brattleboro, he was likely to reach into his coat pockets for money and find only a jackknife or a scarred golf ball.

At first, many neighbors—hardscrabble farmers or tradespeople—deemed Kipling's behavior merely odd and reclusive. Then Carrie Kipling persuaded the government to set up a private post office at Naulakha to accommodate the stacks of royalty checks and other correspondence flowing to the couple's estate, and some locals grumbled that the golf-loving writer was putting on airs. To them, Rudyard Kipling's afternoon rounds at Naulakha suggested an upper-crust gent with too much time on his hands, and they likely figured that with the first snowfall, the Englishman would have to put away his clubs. But they reckoned without considering Kipling's passion for the game and his pronounced case of "cabin fever." When the harsh winter of 1893–94 struck, Kipling peered at his buried meadow and painted his white gutta-perchies red. Then he bundled up, shouldered his kit of clubs, tramped outside with tin cans in hand, stepped off suitable distances for holes, and jammed the cans into the snow. He fashioned a small tee of the white stuff, balanced a scarlet ball on it, and launched the first teeth-chattering stroke of snow golf.

On that frigid day and many more to follow, Kipling wrote all morning and tripped through the snow with clubs and balls in the afternoon, the sound of "guttie" clinking against tin sweet music to his ears. Sometimes, when new powder blanketed Naulakha, he strapped on snowshoes and, as he hacked and stumbled from tin cup to tin cup, sharpened his skill in how to fall properly in a half-sitting, half-kneeling manner. He picked himself up each time, brushed off the snow, squinted through his frost-rimmed spectacles for his lie, and selected a club.

Throughout his Vermont sojourn, Kipling played snow golf even on days that he described in a letter to a friend as filled with "knife-edged cold . . . a cloudless sky, a sun grinning like a skull, and a wind that ripped the bones off you." His pastime furnished Vermonters proof that mad dogs and Englishmen went out not only in the noonday sun, but also in the noonday snows. While neighbors found Kipling's winter rounds further evidence of his foreign ways, not even the most puzzled locals could argue that, amid those chilly rounds at Naulakha, he obviously did some effective literary plotting.

Kipling played his last round at Naulakha in 1896, before sailing for England. He fully intended to return to his beloved Vermont home, but his daughter died in 1899, and he found himself unable to abide the thought of Naulakha without her. He never visited the United States again.

Among American golfers in northern climes, the English author's forays into Naulakha's snow and ice proved nearly as memorable a legacy as his immortal books for children. So popular had his winter pastime become by the turn of the century that the fledgling USGA not only crowned him the king of snow golf but also codified rules for the game, even passing edicts against cheating by shivering sportsmen.

Today, for many, winter golf means a junket to sun-kissed Southern courses. But on snow-encased fairways and greens above the Mason-Dixon Line, diehards desperate for a fix of club and ball can still be spotted punishing red, orange, and other brightly hued balls that few golf purists would ever dream of using except in the snow. The sight is Rudyard Kipling's links legacy.

Southbound

On New Year's Day 1898, ten golfers showed up at a resort to compete in America's first professional tournament "down south," but not on some sun-drenched Florida fairway. The players slipped and stumbled across a frozen patch of turf in Lakewood in southern New Jersey, in pursuit of a $150 purse.

Brothers Ed and Val Fitzjohn and the other eight players had carried their clubs to the Ocean County Hunt and Country Club, a compound of hotels and two golf courses, to compete not only for the money, but also for choice head professional jobs throughout the Northeast.

In the January 2, 1898, *New York Times,* a columnist wrote: "The meeting was one of the golfing giants, to each of whom was granted an unknown degree of skill and each of whom had their particular partisans. The purse offered an incentive which invited their best efforts."

Although many Gay Nineties socialites boarded luxury trains clattering farther south than Lakewood, an affluent crowd gathered to watch the tourney, touted by the *Times* as "a sporting event of greater interest than any that has been held here [in Ocean County]." Their choice of chilly, pine-shrouded Lakewood instead of one of the popular hotels and courses in Hot Springs, Virginia, Augusta, Georgia, and Jacksonville, Florida, reflected a fad for winter resorts among America's blue bloods. Although skiing was not yet in vogue and mountain resorts in Vermont and Colorado had little tug on the wealthy's wallets, society doctors extolled the health benefits of bracing walks on snowy woodland paths and dips in the frigid Atlantic. Any fashionable Eastern resort with snow and sea would do, and operators of the Ocean County Club, battling for patrons' dollars with other winter sanctuaries, had staged several successful amateur tournaments in which guests had played. So had other resorts. With golf's popularity spreading and with the rich patrons' own clubs competing to sign professionals as instructors, what better way to lure new business, the Ocean County entrepreneurs decided, than to showcase crack golfers at the already popular resort?

At Lakewood on New Year's Eve 1897, over a hundred of the nation's wealthiest swells and their wives drank champagne and waltzed across the ballroom of the Ocean County Club in tuxedos and costly gowns. Next morning the guests forced themselves out of bed, shook off the effects of the previous night's revelries, and dressed warmly for the tournament. Some of the men filled silver or gold flasks with spirits to ward off the chill.

The morning imbibers needed only to scan *The New York Times*'s weather report to reach for their first nip:

"Indications . . . are light snow in morning, followed by fair, cold wave, north to northwest gales."

The men who had to rip balls into those winds read the weather report too and dressed accordingly: overcoats, thick woolen scarves and mufflers, and hunting-style caps that covered the ears. Several of the golfers wore gloves to prevent frostbite, a sage choice considering the tournament's format—a one-day, thirty-six-hole marathon.

By twilight, two players remained on the frozen-solid course, the nearly gale-force winds lashing them and the hundred or so shivering spectators. The Fitzjohns had tied at the end of two rounds with scores of 92 and 88, high under normal conditions but creditable on the frozen course, where putts that did not hit the cup dead center skidded away thirty feet or more. The brothers teed off in the first play-off hole, and Val beat Ed to pocket the winner's share of $75.

The Lakewood tournament proved far more than testimony that turn-of-the-century golfers' mania for the game rivaled that of any succeeding generation. The Ocean County Hunt and Country Club's use of a professional golf tournament as commercial bait to lure free-spending millionaires to the grounds outlined the course of the golf resort business. Within twenty years, Caribbean and Californian courses would sell sun and fun to duffers, but frigid Lakewood could lay claim to the title of America's first winter golf getaway.

Inside Moves

In January 1911, thuds echoed from a New York warehouse. Outside the concrete walls, snow shrouded the streets, but that did not stop local golfers. Those strange smacks puzzling passersby were the sounds of golf balls slapping against canvas curtains, or "pockets," an entrepreneurial golf professional's remedy for winter-weary hackers' cabin fever.

In 1910, Tom Wells, a journeyman professional golfer in the New York City area, had pitched not only golf balls, but also an idea for indoor golf. Many of his students had lamented that once winter arrived, they could only stuff their clubs in a closet and pray for an early thaw. A working-class man himself, Wells knew that Southern golf vacations were for the rich only, but that the players cramming the Northeast's public courses, the "ordinary Joes," also had an inordinate passion for the game. So Wells devised his solution for local duffers' seasonal blues—indoor golf.

Wells and several backers had pooled some cash to rent a warehouse with ten thousand square feet of floor space, which he converted into a golf arena with not an inch of grass, but with gargantuan canvas pockets lined up in rows throughout the building. In arena golf, players blasted tee shots at the pockets; an approximate distance estimating how far the ball would have traveled if the canvas had not smothered the stroke was gauged by Wells's staff of so-called spotters, whose guesses on yardage were law. The players followed their drives with walks to a series of artificial greens with putters in hand.

With no grass, no sun, no wind, no rain, no bunkers, and a gloomy old warehouse, arena golf offered players little of the genuine article except the most important thing: the chance to put club to ball in winter. Wells's idea proved a hit in New York, golfers waiting in the cavernous warehouse for hours for a chance to whack a few drives and push a few putts. Wells and other entrepreneurs opened other indoor courses throughout the state and held matches between teams, or winter clubs, from various cities.

For a few years, Wells turned a profit, but with the nation's entry into World War I in 1917, the government needed every available inch of warehouse space, and indoor golf's major material, canvas, was needed for aircraft fuselages and other military uses. Wells's warehouses shut their doors to winter golfers and never reopened.

For a few years, Wells's canvas-filled arenas had given Northern golfers a partial antidote to cabin fever. Tom Wells's canvas dream came and went—but it would come back, bigger and more lucrative than ever, in the 1990s with indoor golf complexes where snow-hating hackers drive balls against canvas screens that feature virtual images of the world's most famous courses.

2

What's in a Name?

Wild Bill

Sporting a cowboy hat, broad-shouldered William Melhorn swaggered onto the Tour in the 1920s and earned a nickname that fit his Western visage—Wild Bill. But the sobriquet did not reflect some two-fisted, tobacco-chewing image; though self-confident, Melhorn was an even-tempered and popular player. The name did reflect the fear that his big drives and complete game stoked in other players, for when he "went wild" on the course, he blew away his competition with subpar rounds. As several Tour greats of the era noted, Melhorn could play two or three mediocre rounds and still destroy the field with one eighteen-hole spree.

Melhorn's first eye-opening burst came on the final day of the Western Open, a major for the players until the Masters' birth, in 1924, when he charged past Al Watrous in a display of shotmaking that featured everything from three-hundred-yard drives to astonishing escapes from sand traps and rough. Although Melhorn finished third in the 1924 U.S. Open, Hagen, Sarazen, Jones, and the other dominant players constantly tracked his rounds, asking

USGA

William Melhorn, whose "wild" birdie blitzes in the 1920s earned him the nickname "Wild Bill."

reporters if the rangy golfer was going wild. Hagen beat Melhorn in a tense final at the 1925 PGA championship, producing a memorable eagle on the first hole to thwart a charge by Wild Bill.

Although Melhorn won twenty-one tournaments, he never nabbed a U.S. Open, a British Open, or a PGA Championship, causing some writers to label him one of the greatest golfers who never won a major. His fellow players hung no such label on him. Ben Hogan considered Wild Bill Melhorn one of the better shot-makers the Tour had ever seen, a man who forced the best players to lift the level of their own games.

The *Real* Tony Manero

The crowd's eyes tracked his every move. Tony Manero was strutting his stuff, poised to grab the winner's check in the biggest competition of his life. But this Tony Manero was not the John Travolta character swaggering beneath the glittering globe on the dance floor of *Saturday Night Fever*. In June 1936, in the fading sunlight of Baltusrol Golf Club's Upper Course, the real-life Tony Manero was in a position few other PGA players and the gallery had thought possible, for the journeyman professional stood within one hole of winning the U.S. Open.

Small, thin Tony Manero had won six tournaments in the late 1920s and early 1930s, but his game did not scare the Walter Hagens and the Gene Sarazens and had not ever brought the thirty-one-year-old Manero within striking distance of a major. But his playing partner that day at Baltusrol exhorted Manero to forget about anything except the final hole. Gene Sarazen understood better than most the long odds that Manero had faced just to qualify for PGA events. Both men were sons of poor Italian immigrants, and both had caddied for years in Westchester County, New York, for nickels and dimes and the chance to play the game. Sarazen's talent far exceeded that of his diminutive friend; Manero had earned his way into the PGA ranks several years after the twenty-year-old Sarazen stunned the sports world by winning the 1922 U.S. Open.

On the final day of the 1936 Open, Manero had started four strokes behind leader "Lighthorse" Harry Cooper and already figured to finish in the money for the tourney. Sarazen also began within striking distance, but "the Squire's" best game did not show up, and by the time he and Manero made the turn to the back nine, Sarazen had fallen from contention. He still saw a chance at victory—for his friend. Winner of the two Opens, Sarazen could tell Manero how it was done.

Manero had scorched the front nine in 33 and had kept up the pace through seventeen. As he and Sarazen walked onto the eighteenth tee, Manero held a two-stroke lead over Cooper. His adrenaline pumping, he was eager to launch his drive.

Ahead of the twosome stretched a long, undulating par-five. A stream and a tall stand of trees flanking the right side deep were certain to swallow Manero's chances if he sliced his ball. Manero reached for his driver, but an official told him to wait for the twosome on the green to finish.

Five minutes later, Manero still waited, starting to pace and to fidget with his club. Sarazen moved with him and talked softly the

The Ralph W. Miller Golf Library

Tony Manero, who won the 1936 U.S. Open, was one of the longer champions in the tournament's history.

entire time. Another five minutes passed. Finally, the official told Manero to tee it up. Manero, not normally a long hitter, crushed a drive down the left border of the hole, and the shot landed just inside the fairway and nestled there.

Manero had passed his first test, but his second shot, a long iron, would require even steadier nerves, the sort that his playing partner possessed. Once again, Sarazen encouraged Manero to take a firm stroke and not court a mistake by pushing the ball.

Manero took a full cut and hit the shot of his career to the edge of the green, safely away from the trees. The crowd, caught up in the underdog's story, erupted, imploring him to hole a long putt for an eagle.

Manero, the cheers ringing around him, walked to the green as Sarazen trailed him by a few steps, allowing him to bask in a moment that even some of the finest players would never savor. But Manero had not won yet.

Manero reached the green, took his time reading its break, and made his choice to ignore the crowd's cries to go right for the hole. He coaxed his first putt within four feet and calmly tapped in his second for the win. To the names of Sarazen, Jones, and other greats of the Open, Tony Manero added his own.

Manero never contended for another major title, but when his one chance had come, he had grasped it. Many players who would win more tournaments and more money than he did could never make the same claim. But more 1990s golf fans can identify John Travolta's Tony Manero than the real one, the one who seized a U.S. Open, among the longest long shots in the tournament's history.

The Other Palmer

Palmer charged toward the PGA's thirty-six-hole record for the lowest score. Long drives, steady iron play, and firm putts—his arsenal brought cheers from the gallery and resignation from the field. He had carded a 60 the previous day and was working on another round in the low 60s, his smile creasing his tanned features with each well-struck shot. Once again, *Johnny* Palmer—not Arnold—was on a roll.

On any given round, the *other* Palmer could dazzle PGA stars and galleries alike. In 1947, eight years before young Arnold Palmer won his first professional tournament, the 1955 Canadian Open, Johnny Palmer seized the notice of the golf world with a four-day burst of birdies that pushed him to victory in the Western Open, no longer a major event but still one of the Tour's most prestigious. He shot a record-shattering 270 for seventy-two holes. While serving as a gunner on a B-29 in World War II, he could only dream of such a moment, for which he had honed his game on the courses in and around Bodine, North Carolina.

Compact, with a sound set of swing mechanics, Palmer possessed a complete tee-to-green game. He showcased it in the 1949 Masters, heading into the final round atop the leaderboard by one stroke, poised, after three days of superb play, to claim his first major. "Eight times during the final round," the Associated Press reported, "the countryside reverberated with the cheers of the multitude as one of the South's favorite sons rapped that ball into the hole to hit that jackpot." The crowd did not roar for the North Carolinian, but for Sam Snead, whose eight-birdie blitz produced a 67 and tumbled Palmer from his chance at Augusta's famed green blazer.

In May 1949, Palmer's opportunity for revenge arrived as he and Snead walked to the first tee of the Hermitage Country Club, in Richmond, Virginia. Both had stormed through grueling match play for a crack at the PGA Championship, and the major lay open to Palmer if he could muster one of his sub-subpar rounds. Snead, with a gallery of fellow Virginians exhorting him on, turned one bad lie after another into one amazing recovery after another during the twosome's thirty-six-hole duel and bested Palmer again, three and two.

In August 1949, the former Army Air Force gunner recovered to win retail magnate George S. May's lucrative World Championship. Palmer went on to win other tourneys on the Tour, always a threat to scorch his opponents with rounds in the low 60s. But his eighteen- and thirty-six-hole rampages never lifted him to a major title, never freed him from the rank of great golfers who fell just short in the majors. In 1949, Palmer could not even blame a loss of nerve or of his game in the Masters and the PGA, but only the inspired play of a man who *took* those majors by elevating his game. Sam Snead would do the same to countless other fine golfers.

On July 2, 1949, about a month after Snead buried Johnny Palmer's dreams of winning a major, a nineteen-year-old Wake

Forest University golfer stormed to victory in the NCAA Championship, in Ames, Iowa. Another Palmer—Arnold—would win those majors that had eluded Johnny.

Jack and the Giant

Would he be "destiny's darling"? A reporter posed the question as a lean, handsome Iowan strode up to the eighteenth tee in the final round of the 1955 U.S. Open, for the golfer had a slim chance to beat the game's best player or to force a Monday play-off with him.

With a Hollywood smile, the challenger looked like a golfer whose chiseled visage had graced magazine covers and guest shots in movies. But he had appeared neither on covers nor in movies, unlike the man whose name stood at the top of the Open's leaderboard. To the Associated Press, the player trying to shove his way into first place was "the darkest of dark horses," "a man practically unknown in the world of sports."

The above scene seems straight out of the movie *Tin Cup*, in which Kevin Costner's driving-range professional comes out of nowhere and bucks the longest possible odds to arrive at the eighteenth of the Open's final round with a chance to score one for underdogs everywhere. Unlike Costner's character, thirty-two-year-old Jack Fleck was real. At the time he launched his drive on the narrow, par-four eighteenth of the 1955 U.S. Open, at the Olympic Club, near San Francisco, few people outside of his hometown, Davenport, Iowa, had ever heard of Fleck.

Jack Fleck described his path to the PGA as a rough road. As a youth in Iowa, he fell in love with the game, and soon after his family moved to Davenport, he began caddying at a local country club. Tom Cunningham, the head professional there, quickly discovered that he had hired a tireless, enthusiastic "looper" (caddie) whose engaging smile made him a favorite of local players. Cunningham soon learned something else: young Jack Fleck could not only carry clubs, but also swing them. Early in the morning and at dusk, Fleck drove, chipped, and putted countless balls across the Davenport Country Club, and dreamed that he might someday crack the PGA's ranks.

His dreams notwithstanding, Fleck approached his love of golf with a practical attitude. Even if he were never to make an impact on the Tour, he could still make a living by becoming a club professional like his mentor, Cunningham. On the day after Fleck graduated from Davenport High School, where he had starred on the golf team, he went to work full-time at the country club, and he worked his way up to a PGA-status instructor.

Golf not only provided Fleck a living, but also introduced him to a stunning young woman named Lynn Burnsdale. An avid player, the Chicago resident was visiting family in Davenport and walked into the local pro shop with a broken club in hand. There she found Jack Fleck at work. They married in 1950 and settled down in Davenport, Jack soon taking a job running the Duck Creek and Credit Island courses. A year later they had a son, and the proud father, wanting his newborn to have a real golf name, asked his wife if they could name him Snead Hogan Fleck after two of the game's best, Sam Snead and Ben Hogan. Lynn Fleck loved golf, but to a point. The couple compromised: Jack gave Lynn a list of every U.S. Open champion, and from the roster of golfing greats she built the name Craig Wood Fleck.

Although Lynn Fleck had quashed her husband's effort to hang "Snead Hogan" on their son, she did encourage the club professional to bring those star players into his life in a different way. "I didn't want Jack ever to have to regret that he might have been a champion [on the PGA Tour]," she would say to a *New York Times* reporter, "so I insisted that he play to get that chance. I'm happy that I made that decision."

What that decision entailed was Lynn Fleck's managing Credit Island and Duck Creek while her husband loaded his clubs in the car and drove to Tour qualifiers and events all across the country. He would always credit his wife for allowing him to take a shot at the big leagues.

Practical-minded locals must have wondered about the Flecks' choice, especially when, over five years, Jack Fleck won only two minor opens and a grand total of $7,400 in forty-one events—an average of barely $180 per tournament. Still, he kept grinding away on the Tour.

Part of the problem, he felt, was that even though he was competing as hard as he could, his divided duties between competition and his job at the Davenport clubs over the years had prevented his becoming as match-tough as full-time Tour players. In comparison to Ben Hogan, Sam Snead, and other PGA stalwarts, Fleck estimated that he was "five to ten thousand rounds behind most of the big-time golfers."

Despite that handicap, Fleck served some notice that his competitive game was coming around in the 1955 season. In fifteen PGA tournaments, he carded an average of 71, always in the money. Few of his fellow golfers, however, did notice. Fewer ever expected his name to sit atop the leaderboards of American golf's crown jewels—the Masters and the U.S. Open. "Good, but a journeyman" was his peers' general consensus.

Shortly after Fleck arrived in San Francisco in June 1955 for the Open, at the Olympic Club, he dashed off a letter to the hometown paper in Davenport: "I gave them my selections for the first ten [on the leaderboard], and I included my name among them as a sleeper." He would have to "wake up"—his best practice round on the gorgeous coastal layout with its treacherous Pacific winds and tricky greens was a 76.

Back at the Flecks' home, Lynn held a slip of paper listing a car and other items that her husband had promised her if he ever won the U.S. Open. In a wire-service interview, she would reveal that "it had been a family joke that whenever she wanted to buy anything, Jack would say, 'Wait until I win the National Open.'" All hopes aside, the idea had always provided the couple with a laugh.

On June 18, 1955, as Jack walked up to the tenth tee of the tourney's last round, neither he nor Lynn was laughing at the notion. He had shot a scintillating 33 on the tough front nine, two under for the round and only one stroke behind Hogan's pace after his front nine. Suddenly, on the eighteenth, cheers erupted from the dense gallery following Hogan. Fleck knew the din's meaning: "the Hawk" had finished strong. The victory party for Hogan's record fifth U.S. Open was commencing—on the assumption that Fleck would not make a charge down the back nine. Although he was but one stroke behind for the moment and the only player with even a prayer of catching Hogan, few in the field or among the gallery gave Fleck any chance at all.

Someone in the gallery mentioned to Fleck that if he netted just one birdie on the back nine, he could tie Hogan. Gene Littler, one of the Tour's finest players and a quick wit, turned to the fan and quipped: "He'll need a few pars, too." Fleck knew the magic number—a 67 just to tie.

On holes ten through thirteen, Fleck played steadily, but on the fourteenth, he flew his approach shot over the green. He was fortunate just to bogey the hole and fall two strokes behind Hogan. The unknown municipal-course professional had only four holes to catch the Hawk. And the narrow eighteenth had bedeviled the field throughout the tournament.

When news of Fleck's brutal fourteenth reached Hogan and the players and press swarming him in the clubhouse, Tour star Gene Sarazen pronounced Hogan the winner over nationwide radio. Among the listeners coast to coast was Lynn Fleck, in Davenport.

Hogan, also sensing that he had become the first to win five Opens, handed Joe Dey, executive director of the United States

Golf Association, the ball Hogan had holed on the eighteenth. "This is for Golf House [Museum]," Hogan said. He had already packed up his clubs.

Out on the fifteenth, Fleck conceded nothing. Defying reporters who thought that "the pressure had seemed to envelop" him on the fourteenth and had reduced his hopes "to the vanishing point," he stormed back with a birdie.

Fleck played smartly but conservatively on the sixteenth and seventeenth for a pair of pars. He then walked up to the eighteenth, needing a birdie on the tight hole, which was flanked on both sides by thick rough.

The New York Times stated: "You'd expect a Jack Fleck to shrivel inside and decide that second place was a higher ranking than he had any right to expect."

Fleck thought otherwise. He believed he had earned the right to aim higher after hanging tough for four days of grueling play. Although he realized that playing safely for a second-place finish would net the biggest check of his golfing career and would pay a lot of bills, "this Corn Belt terror went boldly for a birdie on the last hole."

Fleck's drive into the rough on the fairway's left brought groans from a gallery that had swelled during his run at Hogan. The Iowan's gutsy choice had seemingly backfired, and when the news reached the clubhouse, Hogan's supporters relaxed even more.

Fleck now had another tough decision. He could play a safe shot onto the fairway and two-putt for a par, leaving him a stroke behind; or he could launch a dangerous approach right at the flag and risk even a second-place finish. Fleck knew what his idol Hogan would have done in the same spot.

Fleck walked up to his nearly buried lie, reached for his seven-iron, and calmly arched his shot right at the flag. His ball dropped seven feet from the cup.

For a moment, the crowd gaped. Then cheers erupted all

around the smiling Iowan. If he holed his putt, he would tie Hogan and force a Monday play-off.

The putt that Fleck faced was twisting and downhill. As he set up over his ball, those seven feet likely looked like seven miles, but he did not agonize for long. He nudged the ball toward the cup.

Seconds later another roar pealed above the eighteenth and carried to the clubhouse. Someone dashed into the locker room and shouted, "The kid's holed it!"

Ben Hogan beckoned to a clubhouse attendant and pointed at his packed-up clubs. "Put those sticks back in the locker," Hogan said. "It looks like I'll be playing tomorrow."

As Hogan battled his disappointment, Lynn Fleck's phones were ringing off the hook at Duck Creek with friends' and reporters' calls. A stream of local players rushed up to offer her their congratulations. For a few jubilant moments, the Flecks' friends nearly forgot that Jack still had to face one of the great pressure players of all time in an eighteen-hole play-off.

Fleck, after joking with the press a few hours earlier that he had barely enough money to buy a postround hamburger and to make his nightly phone call to Davenport, went to bed early. Next morning, June 19, the biggest of his career, he claimed that he had slept eight sound hours. Whatever emotions churned within him, he had already convinced Arthur Daley, one of America's most prominent sportswriters, that "this nerveless young man of thirty-two, his totally undistinguished career to the contrary, is made of a champion's true-tempered steel." Yet, as Fleck knew, his suddenly burnished image would lose its sheen if his game fell apart against Hogan in the play-off. Many of the game's best had crumbled when head to head against the Hawk.

In Davenport, Lynn Fleck knew that hard fact about name players' collapses against Hogan, but tried to go about business as usual as her husband walked up to Olympic's first tee on June 19, 1955. Despite a pounding rainstorm, she opened the Credit Island pro shop. But when the play-off's tee time neared, she flipped on the club radio and sat down to listen with a handful of friends to the hole-by-hole national broadcast.

On the first hole, Hogan sprayed his drive into the rough, but anyone interpreting that start as an omen that the Hawk would easily fall was wrong. Fleck knew that if he had any chance, he had to attack the greens, and he did, going right for the cup across the testing tracts rather than playing safely for two-putts.

Hogan's supporters hoped that when a rabbit suddenly burst through the crowd and darted past their man on the third tee, the creature might be a lucky rabbit for him. And by the end of seventeen holes, it appeared that might be the case. Hogan, who had trailed by three after ten holes, had cut Fleck's lead to a mere stroke. Few golfers would have bet against the Hawk as the twosome walked onto the eighteenth for what would prove a memorable conclusion.

Hogan, driving first on the 337-yard hole, was determined to birdie it and tried to get something extra on his tee shot. As he coiled into impact, he slipped on a tiny patch of sand, and he hooked his ball into thick, knee-high grass off the fairway.

Fleck banged his drive down the middle. Then Hogan thrashed at his grass-shrouded ball—it traveled *two feet*. He dug at it again, and it moved perhaps three feet, leading one spectator to ask another: "Was that a practice swing or did Hogan miss?"

On his fourth shot, Hogan reached the fairway, and he pitched his fifth onto the green. He knew, however, that unless Fleck collapsed, the chance for a fifth Open was gone.

Fleck pitched his second shot about fifteen feet from the flag. For one of the few times in the past two days, the Iowan could play it safe on the twisting green, facing a two-putt for par and victory.

Although his chances were slim, Hogan conceded nothing, rolling in a thirty-foot putt that brought a deafening cheer from the gallery. Then, to the shock of many observers, Fleck went right for the cup and nearly sank it for a birdie. His ball nestled just a foot away, all that stood between him and a moment he had never truly thought possible.

USGA

Moments later, Jack Fleck tapped in for the victory and claimed a niche in golf's annals as one of the unlikeli-est Open champs ever.

Virtually unknown Iowa club pro Jack Fleck *(right)* refused to fade on the final eighteen of the 1955 U.S. Open and then beat the great Ben Hogan *(left)* in a play-off.

In the ultimate accolade, renowned Tour scribe Linc Werden lauded: "Fleck won by superior golf. There was nothing 'lucky' about it."

Life for the club professional and his wife changed literally overnight. The man who had joked that he was a "sleeper" in the tournament had awakened the golf world to the fact that he could *play.* He was mobbed by reporters, autograph hunters, and busi-nessmen wielding endorsement offers. In New York City on June 26, 1955, Secret Service agents whisked him off to meet the game's number one fan—President Eisenhower. Ike not only congratulated the long-shot champion but invited him and his wife to the White House, where they would visit on July 11.

At the pro shop in Davenport, the Flecks' friends and neighbors unfurled a giant sign with four-foot-high letters proclaiming "Welcome Home, National Open Champ!" On the bridge span-ning the Mississippi between Davenport and Moline, a similar sign appeared.

Of all the honors accorded Fleck, the one that meant the most to him and his wife took place a week after the Open. The people of Davenport turned out to give the hometown hero a triumphal parade and civic dinner. Fleck described the welcome as "a wonderful homecoming" and expressed his hope that he might now find a respite from the publicity. It was not to be—at least not for a few months. "When I finally got home," Fleck said, "I had to take the phone off the hook."

Lynn Fleck added: "Our home became a Davenport version of Grand Central Station. And we have received so many press clippings from people we don't know that we will have enough to bore our friends with for the next twenty-five years."

To Jack Fleck, who, unlike some hard-living colleagues on the Tour, neither drank nor smoked, the only celebration that truly mattered was that with his family and his Davenport friends. When asked about her husband's meteoric victory, Lynn's sense of humor curtailed any chance of her husband's getting "a big head": "He had to win to pay for all the telephone calls," she said.

Jack Fleck would play well on the Tour over the next few years, winning a tournament in California and pushing Arnold Palmer hard in the 1961 U.S. Open. But at home, he remained just plain Jack, the neighbor who had just happened to electrify the sports world in 1955. Unlike Kevin Costner's future celluloid golfer in *Tin Cup,* Jack Fleck *did* finish first on the Open's leaderboard, and he did so by vanquishing one of the sport's true giants.

Today, Jack Fleck owns and runs a small course in Arkansas. His first wife, Lynn, passed away in 1971. Tucked away in a corner of his home are the Hogan-brand clubs with which he defeated their namesake in the 1955 U.S. Open.

3

The Law and the Links

Kolf, Anyone?

In 1652, a clubhead's click against a small ball sounded a milestone round in the New World. Several men wielding crooked wooden clubs putted around the town green. But the colonists were not transplanted Scotsmen. The men playing the first recorded round of colonial golf were Dutch, and their makeshift course undulated across the common green of New Amsterdam (later New York City). They called their game *kolven,* or *kolf.*

Five years later, in 1657, a threesome of kolfers knocked a ball around the dirt paths of Fort Orange (now Albany). Lining up their shots, discussing local affairs, they were startled by the sudden appearance of the settlement's sheriff. He held a written complaint signed by other colonists dismayed not that the trio were playing kolf, but that they were doing it on a Sunday and might damage fences and back windows.

The sheriff told the offenders to pick up their kolf balls, shoulder their clubs, and sin no more on the Sabbath.

In 1659, evidence that local kolfers still defied sheriffs' bans of the game appeared in a Colonial Dutch ordinance: "The Honorable Commissary and Magistrates of Fort Orange and the Village of Beverwyck [in present-day New York], having heard divers [diverse] complaints from the burghers of this place against the practice of playing kolf along the streets, which causes great damage to the windows of the houses and also exposes people to the danger of being injured and is contrary to the freedom of the public streets. Therefore, their honors, wishing to prevent same, hereby forbid all persons to play kolf in the streets, under penalty of forfeiture of 25 florins for each person who shall be found doing so."

Although the round's end marked the first ban on Sunday golf in America, the injunction would hardly prove the last. Clerics and churchgoers' campaigns to stamp out Sunday golf would flourish well into the twentieth century.

The question for generations of golf purists was not whether some high-spirited Dutchmen enjoyed a game of kolf in 1650s New York. The question was whether kolf was real golf. The answer is that, at best, kolf was a colonial form of *miniature* golf, not the real game.

While Dutch linksters have long claimed that golf was invented on the Netherlands' frozen canals in the thirteenth century, Scots can irrefutably counter that *their* ancestors were smacking balls as early as A.D. 1100 around Perth and many other sites from coast to Highlands. As any Scottish golfer can point out and as historian Robert Browning chronicled, "Scots devised [golf's] essential features . . . the combination of hitting for distance with the final nicety of approach to an exiguous mark, and the independent progress of each player with his own ball, free from interference by his adversary." This was the game that Scots and Englishmen brought to various colonial tracts—not the miniature kolf played by the Dutch. Dutch artists of the seventeenth and eighteenth centuries painted scenes of players stroking balls across canals and their banks alike, but *het kolven* bore far more resemblance to curling than to golf. The Dutch used just one crooked club; the Scots had a bagful.

Historically speaking, the Scots stand first on the links and first on the leaderboard—both in the Old and the New World.

Until Death Do Us Part

On September 7, 1729, colonial governor William Burnet's workload finally killed him. He left behind two loves, his wife, Mary, and his golf game. His will's mention of "Nine Golf Clubs, One Iron Ditto, and Seven Dozen Balls" was the first official evidence that Scottish-style golf had materialized in the Thirteen Colonies.

Long before American politicians from William H. Taft to Bill Clinton sought a few hours' sanctuary on the links from affairs of state, William Burnet worked out his bureaucratic frustrations by whacking balls across tracts of colonial New York, New Jersey, and Massachusetts. Boston's Puritans, especially dour Cotton Mather and Salem witch trials judge Samuel Sewall, frowned on such frivolous pursuits, but Burnet feared no cleric's or jurist's wrath. And with good reason: he was the godson of King William and Queen Mary.

With his royal godparents looking on in 1688, Burnet was christened not only into the Church of England, but into a life of privilege. Athletic and high-spirited, he was a poor student whom the faculty of Cambridge University booted from campus for lazy, unruly habits such as cutting classes, quaffing ale, and chasing tavern maids.

Three passions governed young Burnet's life—the links; highborn, attractive ladies; and the law. The last brought stability to his life, as he studied under several barristers and was called to the bar in his twenties. In 1720, he parlayed his royal connections into a commission as governor of New York and New Jersey.

When servants lugged the baggage of the new royal dignitary onto the town dock of New York on September 16, 1720, they took special care with Burnet's golf kit and balls. For the next nine years, colonists would spot their governor, squinting beneath his shoulder-length periwig, his costly buckled shoes spread around a golf ball, in muddy pastures lining up a clubhead to a "featherie" (feather-stuffed leather ball) to hack away political woes for an hour or two.

A sophisticated, kindly, talented legislator, Burnet was also a convivial golfer any modern player would welcome to a foursome. History does not record who played with the governor, but his ownership of seven dozen balls, a costly collection in the era, proved that he played often, and an artist's depiction of Burnet as a man with a pleasant smile reflected a golfer who would have insisted upon on-course company and competitions.

Not even Burnet's escapes with his kit and balls to open acreage from Albany to Boston could ease his post's incessant burdens: the omnipresent threat of French troops in Canada, Mohawk raiders, and self-serving merchants always undercutting his policies. On September 7, 1729, William Burnet died of exhaustion.

Today, every time that cameras capture legislators from presidents on down in the political pecking order on a fairway or a green, the legacy of William Burnet's "Nine Golf Clubs" and "Iron Ditto" lives on.

Accidents Happen

On Thanksgiving morning of 1897, Eddie McCoy staggered into the locker room of the Baltusrol (New Jersey) Golf Club and collapsed.

Several caddies carried the semiconscious forty-seven-year-old to his nearby home, in Millburn, and summoned a doctor. By nightfall, McCoy was dead, and the reported cause set off a furor on editorial pages and in golf clubs throughout the nation: Eddie McCoy, *The New York Times* announced, "had died . . . from the effect of a blow from a golf ball received on the club's links."

McCoy had been a career caddie, and his accidental death terrified private and public courses alike with nightmares of liability issues. "While two or three persons have been killed on the English and Scotch links during the past fifty years in this way, this reported death was the first to be recorded in America," the *Times* reported, "and it caused a decided sensation in consequence."

Several Baltusrol caddies claimed that McCoy had been carrying a bag down one of the fairways and an errant shot from an adjoining hole had rocketed against the side of his skull, and the rock-hard gutta-percha ball had knocked him flat. He lurched to his feet, shouldered the bag of the affluent club member, and finished the man's round, afraid of losing his tip if he sought aid. At the round's end, McCoy had reeled into the clubhouse and toppled to the floor.

Baltusrol's members and those of other millionaires' clubs asserted in the *Times* and other newspapers that "the percentage of danger on links, unless very short and crowded ones, from accidents of this sort was infinitesimally small, notwithstanding the use of the hard gutta-percha balls and the force with which they are driven."

Emphasizing that the Baltusrol course was as safe as any in America, the club's officials publicly questioned the veracity of accounts of McCoy's death and dispatched private investigators to clear up the matter.

Several days after McCoy's death, his fellow caddies retracted their previous accounts. Baltusrol's president informed the *Times* that "the investigation of the matter proved that McCoy had been seized with an epileptic fit in the clubhouse on Thanksgiving morning and died soon after removal to his home."

Although the club refused to elaborate on the investigation, the members assured the reporter that "there was no truth whatever in the story that he [McCoy] had been hit by a golf ball." And how did the club explain the caddie's fatal fractured skull? The simple result of his "fall in the clubhouse," an unfortunate accident with no liability for Baltusrol.

Neither McCoy's family, after discussions with Baltusrol's investigators, nor his fellow caddies said another public word about the incident.

On Strike

On a steamy Saturday in August 1899, the members of the Harbor Hills Golf Club arrived at the clubhouse in their blazers and caps and discovered something missing there—the caddies. The youthful bag-toters had walked off the job at the Staten Island links after club officials had scoffed at the boys' demand for a ten-cent hike in their quarter-per-round wage. Of course, most of the members who sneered at the notion of a pay raise for the caddies rarely if ever tipped them. Harbor Hills players were not alone in their stinginess—it was the norm at most clubs.

To the many businessmen who played Harbor Hills, the word "strike" was anathema, reeking of anarchy, and the last place that tycoons expected to encounter defiant workers was on the course, where members sought a leisurely round and a later round or two in the clubhouse. Without caddies, Harbor Hills' duffers would have to shoulder their own clubs or forgo their game. Most chose the latter option, unwilling to turn their golf into *work*.

As the handful of golfers lugging their own clubs trudged from the clubhouse to the first tee, a din erupted behind the wrought-iron fence that encircled the club. The caddies had walked off the course, according to a *New York Times* reporter, but had gathered outside it, and "hooted and yelled like Indians" at the players, who thought nothing of paying an extra dime or two when liquor prices went up, but refused an additional ten cents for the caddies.

The golfers teed off and headed down the fairway, the boys trailing at a distance behind the fence, their jeers and catcalls incessant.

During the next few weeks, club members attempted to hire other caddies, but local boys would not cross the picket line at the fence, fearing the fists of the striking "loopers." Attendance at the club waned, only the hardiest players being willing to endure the caddies' jibes. Still, the boys' bosses refused to pay the dime.

With the daily insults failing to budge the club's officials, the caddies' youthful negotiators devised a new pressure tactic. Several weekends into the strike, the golfers inured to the adolescent heckling showed up for a round and discovered that every hole's flag and cup had vanished and that the club's cache of pricey balls was empty.

The members reacted as they did when faced with work stoppages at their factories. They summoned the police.

As the boys laughed at the players who had no flags to aim at and no balls to strike even if they had a target, several dozen New Brighton policemen rattled up to the fence in paddy wagons, waded with billy clubs into the crowd, tossed boys into the wagons, and hauled nine of them to jail.

In a statement to the *Times,* Captain Otto Hockmeyer huffed that "where the matter will end is not known," but he hoped that "with the ringleaders arrested, the other boys will abandon the fight and come to terms."

The teenage "ringleaders" and their fellow strikers disappeared from their clubhouse perch but refused to report to work. Once again, the club tried to hire new caddies and found none willing to cross the regular loopers.

Finally, the club's board sat down at the bargaining table with the boys, the latter group in knickers and worker's caps, their bosses in costly suits and stiff collars. The officials told the boys that they could have their jobs back—without a raise. The caddies countered that the members could continue their rounds and carry their own bags, or hire other caddies, if possible.

After the board, infuriated by the ongoing stubbornness of the boys, went behind closed doors, the members emerged with a counteroffer of a nickel raise per round. The caddies grumbled at the compromise, but accepted. In the words of one writer, the men and women of Harbor Hills Golf Club had learned a hard lesson in the difference between recreation and manual labor on the course.

The Road to Ruin

Mrs. Darwin S. James spent her life sniffing out "evil," and she believed that on Sundays, one should spend one's time in church and with family—period. As president of the Women's Sabbath Alliance, the middle-aged wife, mother, and crusader had simply forgotten how to have fun, critics charged. In 1900, she responded with a stepped-up campaign to make sure no one else had fun on Sundays and fixed her social sights on the so-called spreading evil of Sunday golf.

In the newspapers, Mrs. James assured golfers that she had nothing against their game, only against their Sunday rounds. She professed that once duffers "listened to reason"—her reason—they would realize that golf on the Sabbath was ruining family life and mocking God, and would tee off on Saturdays instead.

Sunday golfers were not the only group under fire from the Women's Sabbath Alliance. Mrs. James was demanding that all newspapers cease printing Sunday editions, as only the Bible was fit reading that day and as publishers were forcing newsboys to work on Sundays, imbuing them with disrespect for the Sabbath and sending them down "the road to perdition."

Mrs. James's concern about the paperboys' sinful Sundays led her back to the links and to their caddies. To the New York papers, she declared: "It isn't so bad for golfers themselves as for the caddies, who are forced to begin doing wrong by working on Sundays at the very outset of their lives. All criminals start on the downward path by working on Sundays."

She did not blame the "problems" on the caddies, most of whom came from poor families and had to grasp any chance to make a dollar or two. Against the men and women prying the youths from church (or so she imagined from her rarefied social circle) Mrs. James railed: "If golfers only considered that they were starting their caddies in a life of sin by making them work on Sunday, they would soon give up their Sabbath day games. . . . Crime is increasing here a great deal faster than the population. Great Britain is the only country in the world where crime is on the decrease. That is because it is the only country in the world where the Sabbath is observed."

Mrs. James offered no proof that caddies sprouted into convicts. And she was waging a losing battle. Even as she harangued sand-wedge sinners, public courses such as Van Cortlandt Park, in New York, teemed with Sunday golfers waiting two hours or more to get the first tee. Although blue laws technically banned a Sunday round, the fact that blue bloods and the middle classes alike were embracing Sunday golf compelled constables and courts to look the other way.

Never on a Sunday

As Benjamin Adams tracked his ball across the sun-splashed Saegkill Golf Club on June 2, 1901, several police officers strode down the fairway. Adams suddenly realized that they were coming toward him.

The policemen surrounded him and "disarmed" him—of his golf clubs. Then they informed him he was under arrest.

The gaping middle-aged golfer, a well-known New York trial attorney, demanded to know the charge. As they hauled him off to a cell, the officers informed him that he had violated a three-week-old law banning golf on Sunday.

On the very morning of Adams's arrest, the Reverend John Havemeyer preached against Sunday golfers from the pulpit of the Central Methodist Church in Yonkers. Just a few blocks away lay one of America's first golf courses, John Reid's St. Andrew's. As Havemeyer's golf-loving parishioners slouched in their pews absorbing his tirade, the cleric did not yet know that the crusade he and many other New York ministers had launched against all Sunday sports, but especially golf, was headed to the courts.

One of Havemeyer's flock stood up during the sermon and challenged him to cite even one Scriptural passage banning Sunday golf.

Havemeyer huffed that he did not have to dignify sacrilegious Sunday golf with an answer.

A day later, Havemeyer and fellow loathers of the links had plenty to say to the press about Sunday golf.

Adams's fellow brethren of Sunday rounds rallied to his cause, wealthy golf-playing New Yorkers threatening to pull themselves and their hefty contributions from churches opposed to Sunday golf and to join more tolerant ministers' flocks. Two clerics among New York City's richest churches immediately renounced their support of the golf ban, claiming that they had not thought the bill through and that as long as worshipers attended Sunday services, a Sabbath round was fine with them.

Havemeyer did not bail out on the bill, nor did dozens of other ministers. They urged the police to arrest other Sunday golfers and voiced their confidence that a jury of respectable citizens would slap Adams with a stiff but legally unspecified fine for breaking the Sabbath as he tried to break par.

Adams, irate that he had spent June 2 in a cell because no judge was available to release him on personal recognizance on a Sunday, turned to a formidable friend and fellow attorney for help. Joseph F. Daly was an advocate renowned for his folksy courtroom witticisms that bored in on a case's most salient point. In a *New York Times* interview on Thursday June 6, 1901, the eve of Adams's trial, Daly hinted at the strategy that he would employ: "To keep the Sunday as these good people [Havemeyer and company] wish us to keep it would be to put us in the boots of the small boy who sat on his mother's knee and was told that if he was good all the time, he would surely go to Heaven.

'But what is Heaven?' asked the little chap.

'Why, Heaven, darling, is a place where it is always Sunday,' the fond mother announced.

'I guess—I guess I'd rather go to the other place then,' the boy decided."

Daly would argue that clerics had every right to tell their parishioners how to get to Heaven, but no right to expect the law to enforce religious edicts against citizens' freedom to choose their Sunday pastime, whether church services or the links.

When Daly and Adams walked into the New York Superior Court building on June 7, 1901, they waded into a mob of fellow golfers shouting their support, ministers and temperance sorts glowering at them, and reporters. Then, Judge Charles Kellogg, a conservative, religious judge, took the bench, called the court to order, and summoned the six jurors.

Laughter from Adams's supporters greeted the jury's arrival— one of the men wore knickers, stockings, and a blazer: golf garb. Kellogg immediately dismissed the juror, seated an alternate, and ordered the trial to commence.

The prosecutor opened with a broad argument that Sunday golf was a harbinger of social decline and must be banned for morality's sake. After a few minutes of this, Kellogg cut the attorney off and barked at him to present the legal issues. As a reporter noted, the prosecution's grounds shrank to the controversial ordinance against Sunday sports and clerics' disapproval of anyone having fun on the Sabbath.

Daly, clad in one of his characteristically loud suits and a checked vest adorned with a gold pocket watch, countered the charges in his affable manner, stopping to smile at the jurors from time to time, running his hand through his thick silver hair whenever punctuating a point. He assailed the Sunday blue law as an unconstitutional blend of church and state. Even if one believed that the edict had merit, Daly argued, it could only apply to *public* courses—not private courses sanctioned to form their own rules.

Seeing where Daly was headed, the prosecution shouted an objection that the law governed all courses, but Kellogg denied the remonstrance. Daly, grinning, reminded the jury that Adams belonged to Saegkill, a private club.

Early in the afternoon, Kellogg instructed the jury and sent them out to deliberate. They filed back into the courtroom forty-five minutes later. Would Sunday golf be saved? wondered a reporter.

The jury foreman soon answered the question: "We, the jury, find the defendant, Adams, not guilty, and we recommend that the existing law in regard to the observation of the Sabbath on the first day of the week be repealed or so amended as not to interfere with the innocent amusement of the citizens of this state on that day."

Cheers erupted from Adams's friends. The band of ministers and their supporters stomped from the court and waited on the main staircase for the reporters. Back inside, spectators swarmed Adams and Daly, hugging them, shaking hands, and slapping backs.

The antigolf backlash began in the evening editions of the newspapers and escalated two days later, Sunday, June 9, 1901, when the Reverend Mr. Havemeyer and other ministers took to their pulpits. As expected, Havemeyer blasted the verdict as an affront to God and morality.

Similarly, a *Times* article reported, the Reverend Stuart

MacArthur, of the Calvary Baptist Church, harangued: "The great and prosperous nations of the earth are those who, as a nation, observe Sunday as a sacred day. These are the nations that, according to the Bible's promise, are going up to the high places of the earth."

The same article noted that Father Brady, of St. Joseph's Church, offered a different view of golf's alleged place among society's ills. "The local authorities are straining at the gnat golf and swallowing the camel saloon allowing the saloon to run openly [on Sundays]... that they might turn their attention to the minor offenses called Sunday sports, which do less harm in a cycle of time than the saloons and other vicious resorts [brothels, gambling halls, opium dens] do in an hour."

Nationwide, local ordinances against Sunday golf and countless diatribes from the pulpit stretched deep into the century. Benjamin Adams's trial, however, first sent Sunday golfers to the links free and clear. His ordeal also opened the way to a 1990s television staple of exciting Sunday finishes to PGA and LPGA tournaments. One can only wonder how Havemeyer and MacArthur would have ranted not just at Sunday golf's triumph, but also at the sight of modern clerics squeezing in a round before or after a sermon.

Grand Theft Golf

In summer 1929, two police darted into a clump of trees in New York's Van Cortlandt Park and waited. A burly man decked out in cap and knickers ambled up to the first tee and blasted a long drive down the fairway. He watched his ball roll to a stop, handed his caddie the driver, and looked at the fairway again. His ball had vanished.

Puzzled, he teed up another one and whacked it to virtually the same spot. He turned away for an instant and asked the caddie to mark the ball. The boy replied that he could not—the second ball was gone.

The golfer drove one more ball down the middle. Once again, he could not seem to spot it.

He instructed the caddie to pick up the bag and follow him down the fairway. As they passed the stand of trees, the golfer signaled the two hidden men, and all three dashed past the gaping caddie and plunged into a dense tangle of brush flanking the other side of the fairway.

A few seconds later, the trio reemerged from the shrubbery. Two had a firm hold on a young man, and the other cradled a bulldog who lapped at his face. The golfer ordered the prisoner to empty his pockets. Glaring, the young man deposited seven golf balls on the fairway; teethmarks had scuffed each one.

When pressed to explain, the young man claimed that he was a San Francisco native and nurse who had recently arrived in New York and was earning extra money by searching for lost balls. The golfer—Officer Joseph Cleary, from the local precinct house—suspected that the "nurse's" business was booming: the policeman and his two aides had been assigned to investigate a mysterious epidemic of disappearing golf balls at the course. But a question still confounded Cleary, a question that the suspect, twenty-four-year-old Frank Conroy, answered only with a shrug. How could he move quickly enough to steal the balls without players or caddies spotting him?

As Cleary mulled over the matter, a drive skittered just past the men, someone on the side either oblivious of fairway etiquette or intent on moving the foursome along. Suddenly the bulldog burst from the policeman's grasp, dashed to the ball, clamped its teeth around it, and vanished into the brush, with Cleary's aides giving chase. They returned ten minutes later, hands and faces nicked by branches and thorns. The canine was long gone.

The bulldog's master was not so lucky. A background check revealed that Frank Conroy was a petty thief and a skilled dog trainer. After a brief trial in the West Farms Courthouse, New York magistrate Delagi dispatched Conroy to the workhouse for ten days.

As police led Conroy off, balls were still disappearing at Van Cortlandt Park, replete with sightings of a white bulldog all over the course. The search for the elusive canine went on for months, but the culprit remained on the loose, never to be caught. Eventually, the thefts ceased, leading golfers to believe that someone, possibly a caddie, had adopted the dog and rescued it from the wayward path.

During the bulldog's crime spree, the creature attained local celebrity, newspapers chronicling the exploits, real and imagined, of the "fairway bandit." *The New York Times* found the creature's capers worthy of a place among "all the news that's fit to print." An editor mused: "One cannot but ponder the career that would be open to such an animal if he were shown the evil of his ways and induced to lead an honest life."

The crafty bulldog might well have been born six decades too soon. Who would doubt that Hollywood would have come calling for the cute little criminal?

The Boys Are Back

In April 1932, the women of the Century Country Club, in White Plains, New York, had seen enough and demanded that Charles C. Webster put a stop to it. "It" was the "laborers and old men" whom Webster, director of the local Emergency Work Bureau, had been dispatching to caddy at the fashionable club on weekends. The men's original jobs had vanished in the Depression, and Webster, like many relief workers across the country, had instituted a program to train unemployed men of all ages as caddies.

The Century Club's women, married to wealthy men above the nation's economic chaos and heiresses to their own families' money, recoiled at the very sight of down-on-their-luck men tramping across the course. Even worse, the women complained in a signed petition to Webster, they did not like the workingmen touching expensive clubs, the implication clear—the "caddies" would be tempted to steal and pawn them. The club had dismissed ten young caddies to make room for the plebeian men, and the women demanded that the head professional hire back the youths.

Webster soon received a second complaint, from the club's greens committee—the husbands—who notified him that the unemployed men were not welcome and that the young caddies would be rehired. Although the older caddies had worked out at other country clubs in Westchester County, Webster could not force a private golf course to continue participation in a public-works program. Free to pretend that life went on untouched by the Depression, the members of the Century Country Club welcomed back the youthful caddies—and paid them less than the daily fee Webster's men had earned.

The Caddie's Revenge

On November 10, 1932, eleven-year-old John Simpson sat with his lawyer as Justice Hagarty came back into the Brooklyn courtroom. Teunis S. Fiero, the man who had injured the boy, tensed at the judge's reappearance—the jurist had deliberated for less than an hour.

Fiero stood accused of injuries caused when he had not waited for a fairway of the Pocatello Country Club, in Middleton, New York, to clear and had struck the boy with a drive. Simpson, caddying for another man, had crumpled unconscious to the grass, his cheek shattered and his eye swelling shut. His doctor had testified that the youth had been fortunate to keep his eye, but that his vision was permanently impaired, and a jury had found Fiero guilty of injuring the boy and had awarded him $4,968, a sizable sum in the Depression. Still, few liability experts believed that the verdict and the damages would stand. On every course in America, the unwritten rule, *The New York Times* reported, was that "it is part of a caddy's duty to watch the flight" of any ball within his range of vision.

Justice Hagarty settled himself behind the bench, riffled through a stack of papers, and peered down at Fiero. "My view is that if the plaintiff [Simpson] had been caddying for the defendant," the judge intoned, "there would be no liability for the reason that then it would have been the plaintiff's duty to watch the defendant drive, to watch the ball in flight, and to mark it when it came to rest.

"The defendant would have been justified in assuming that the plaintiff was doing that for which he was being paid and, therefore, there would have been no reason to warn him." According to witnesses, Fiero had never yelled "fore" to warn the boy, but could not have missed seeing him.

"In this case, however," the judge went on, "the boy was not his caddy, and the defendant, even if he had admitted seeing him in the position of danger, would not have been justified in assuming he was watching the play. It must be conceded that although golf may not be deemed a very dangerous game, a driven ball is a dangerous missile and that its flight and direction cannot always be controlled by the player."

As the *Times* related, Hagarty's next words took direct aim at reckless conduct on the course: "These conditions, while adding zest to the game, place upon the player the duty of taking all reasonable precautions to see that no one is injured and make him liable for damage if such precautions are not taken."

Caddies still had to watch their backs on the links, but thanks to the eleven-year-old's suit, golfers who did not pay attention to foursomes in front of them would pay a price.

John Q. Public

In 1948, Baltimore businessman John E. Law was not looking to start trouble on public golf courses. He just wanted to get on the city's best metropolitan links, tired of relegation to a scarred nine-hole course at Carroll Park. He accepted the fact that he lacked the correct skin color to join a good private club, but chafed at the unwritten law that excluded blacks from Mount Pleasant, Clifton, Forest Park, and other stellar public courses within a few miles of his home. Despite friends' warnings to stick with Carroll Park, Law hired an attorney, a white one, to challenge the racist policy of local courses.

On July 13, 1948, Law filed a suit claiming that "the present unqualified, prohibitory" whites-only policy of public links had no basis in law because blacks' tax dollars, as well as whites', paid for and maintained public courses. The defense attorneys' arguments that the clubs did not practice discrimination but merely upheld their right to keep any "undesirables" off public property did not move the judge, who ruled in Law's favor, forcing the courses to admit blacks on the fairways. But the court did not add equality in tee times. Course operators assigned only early or twilight rounds to black golfers for years to come.

Although this was an incomplete decision, Law's crusade spread, a similar suit opening up Louisville's public courses in 1952 and many other cities removing exclusions over the following decades. Law, however, never considered himself a civil rights trail-blazer. In an interview after the verdict, he claimed that his primary motivation was that his game was getting too good for Carroll Park and that he needed to challenge himself on better courses. His family and friends knew differently: years after his death, his daughter said that John Law was fed up with discrimination and had chosen his own battleground carefully and well.

4

A Place in the Sun

The Eye of the Storm

On the morning of July 18, 1896, on eastern Long Island, history strode to the first tee of the U.S. Open. The small wiry eighteen-year-old golfer who gripped his driver and peered down the 275 sun-splashed yards of Shinnecock Hills' opening hole, the Mews, faced obstacles far more formidable than the stiff Atlantic gusts blowing in his face and the windmill that his tee shot needed to clear some seventy-five yards away. For that teenaged golfer, John Shippen, was measuring the first swing of an African-American golfer in a professional tournament.

Shippen knew that on the eve of the 1896 Open, the tournament's white competitors had demanded his banishment, as well as that of Shinnecock Indian Oscar Bunn. Only because of the integrity of Theodore Havemeyer, president of the fledgling United States Golf Association, was Shippen standing on the Mews.

Shippen's journey into the eye of a racist storm began in 1888, when his father, an African-American Presbyterian minister of

Jamaican descent, took a post as a cleric and teacher at the Shinnecock Indian reservation on Long Island. Not long afterward, Scottish golf professionals Willie Davis and then Willie Dunn arrived on the island to design Shinnecock Hills Golf Club, relying largely on Shinnecock Indians for labor and training some of the local youths as caddies for the Southampton club's moguls and mavens. Two of the caddies, Shippen and Bunn, learned to play the game under Dunn's expert tutelage. Shippen soon displayed such shotmaking aptitude that Dunn allowed him to give lessons, making the youth the Scot's assistant pro.

When the USGA selected Shinnecock Hills to host the second U.S. Amateur and U.S. Open, various club members encouraged Shippen and Bunn to enter the latter. No "right-thinking" blue blood of the era would have considered allowing a black or an Indian into the Amateur, the more prestigious of the two events as it catered to the finest players among affluent socialites. Because, however, country club members of the Gay Nineties considered golf pros a highly skilled form of "the help," the notion of Shippen and Bunn pitting their skills against other professionals in the 1896 Open did not strike many at Shinnecock as outlandish, and some of the club's members believed Shippen or Bunn could actually win the Open.

In July 1896, a horde of socialites jammed the graceful verandas of the clubhouse, the work of renowned architect Stanford White, to watch upscale golfers battle in the game's event of the season, the U.S. Amateur. H. G. Whigham captured the title and, along with fellow Chicagoan amateur Charles Blair Macdonald, would compete against the professionals in the Open, slated for the following day. Expecting to tee off in the event with such greats as Horace Rawlins, the 1895 Open champion, were Bunn and Shippen.

The New York Times proclaimed that the Open would prove "hotly contested," but on the day before the championship, a different contest erupted. The mostly foreign-born pros held a meeting, marched up to Havemeyer, and flung the gauntlet of racism in his face by threatening to boycott the Open unless he banned Bunn and Shippen from the competition.

Several versions of what followed between Havemeyer and the disgruntled professionals would emerge. The first and most accepted account depicted Havemeyer brusquely refusing to cut Shippen and Bunn from the field and retorting that the Open would go on—even if the two were the only ones left to play.

The second widely circulated account of Havemeyer's actions would spark speculation about Shippen's heritage. According to several sources, Havemeyer stated that the Open would take place no matter what, but informed the protesters that because Shippen was only one-half black and the other half Shinnecock Indian and because Bunn was a full-blooded Shinnecock, there was no reason to boycott the Open. The account's specious insinuation that the professionals found Indians acceptable, but not blacks, ignored the white players' objections to the presence of *both* a black and an Indian. Regarding Shippen's lineage, in a 1986 interview, his daughter, Clara Shippen Johnson, stated that her father was an African-American, her own mother a Native American.

A few years before his death in a Newark, New Jersey, nursing home in 1968, Shippen himself told a friend that Havemeyer had unequivocally informed the professionals that Shippen would play and that the Open would go on, boycott or not. Yet another scenario asserted that Havemeyer had refused to ban Shippen and Bunn because both were "native-born" Americans, their race notwithstanding.

One fact of the controversy stands undisputed. With remarkable integrity in an era of virulent racism, Havemeyer asserted that the USGA, not the players, ran the Open, and guaranteed that John Shippen would tee off the next day—with or without the recalcitrant professionals.

At ten in the morning of July 18, 1896, more than two dozen golfers, all but two of them white, began teeing off in pairs at the Mews. Havemeyer had won the battle of wills.

Macdonald, the Amateur champion from the year before, was paired with Shippen. Despite his amateur status, Macdonald had developed a stellar game at St. Andrews in Scotland.

Shippen had honed his game at Shinnecock, and as the first of the Open's two rounds unfolded, his knowledge of every bunker and sand-swept hill and the vagaries of the nearby Atlantic's gusts soon materialized. The Belfry, the Crater, the Plateau, the Small Hole, the Cloister, the 356 yards of Shinnecock's longest hole, Longacre, Sandy Mount—these and the rest of the White Course's challenging holes did not hamper the strokes of John Shippen.

On that summer morning, Shippen proved it by carding a 78 to share the first-round lead with four others, including Scots James Foulis and Dunn, Shippen's mentor. Shippen's playing partner, Macdonald, shot an embarrassing 83. Bunn, Shippen's fellow target of racist ire, suffered through a round of 89, his prowess as a long-distance driver helping him little that morning.

In the afternoon, the men who had sought to ban Shippen from the contest faced the challenge of stopping his quest for America's professional championship. Few whites of the day would have lauded Shippen's new status as the first American to lead a professional tournament.

In front of the scarlet-coated club members, Shippen again advanced to the first tee, but alone this time. Macdonald had withdrawn from the event and merely kept Shippen's score the rest of the way.

As on his morning round, Shippen kept pace with Dunn, Rawlins, Foulis, and other favorites, the caddie remaining among the leaders as he approached the thirteenth hole.

Shippen stepped up to the tee and sliced his drive onto a sand-choked road. He failed to recover, rolling in his putt ten strokes later. Racists in the crowd could relax: the nation's first African-American professional was not going to win the Open.

Shippen somehow recovered from his disastrous thirteenth. When he left the eighteenth green, the home hole in front of the

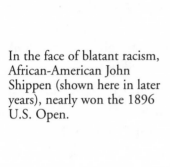

In the face of blatant racism, African-American John Shippen (shown here in later years), nearly won the 1896 U.S. Open.

USGA

clubhouse's crowded veranda, his second-round scorecard read 81. With a final score of 159, Shippen had finished tied for fifth place, seven strokes behind the champion, Foulis—and in the money. Foulis reaped a purse of $200, and Shippen pocketed $10—the first African-American golfer to win prize money in a U.S. Open.

One can only speculate what might have happened if Shippen's touch had not temporarily deserted him at the sandy thirteenth. In one respect, however, Shippen had triumphed. Displaying maturity far beyond his years and foreshadowing the demeanor of baseball's Jackie Robinson some fifty years later, Shippen never flinched amid the sullen field of white professionals and proved he belonged in their midst. He is known to have played in four more U.S. Opens, in 1899, 1900, 1902, and 1913, three years before most professional tournaments officially banned African-American players.

America's first black golf professional, the first American to lead a U.S. Open, and, in all likelihood, America's first bona fide golf professional of any race, John Shippen compiled one landmark after another with dignity and modesty. But of all his achievements, his thirty-five-year tenure as the head professional at America's first black country club, Shady Rest, in Scotch Plains, New Jersey, left one of his most enduring imprints. At the milestone club, Shippen ignited a love for the game in several generations of African-American youths.

Today, at Scotch Hills Golf Course, formerly Shady Rest, PGA club professional John Turnbull and the John Shippen Foundation Scholarship and Youth Golf Program tend Shippen's legacy through memorabilia and an annual John Shippen tournament. With the help of golfing great Lee Elder and director/producer Lawrence Londino's outstanding documentary *A Place for Us,* which chronicles the history of Shady Rest and John Shippen, the story of the trailblazing African-American golfer is spreading.

John Shippen's true legacy lives on.

A Card-Carrying Member

Whenever John D. Rockefeller needed a golf lesson, he headed to the Morris County Golf Club (New Jersey) for a session with an instructor the tycoon considered the best in the business. All of golf's big names of the 1920s and 1930s, from Hagen to Hogan, knew how good Rockefeller's swing coach, Dewey Brown, was.

Several of the game's biggest stars consulted Brown when a sudden hitch appeared in their swing, and Brown, who could belt drives with the longest hitters of the era and could snake a putt into the cup with the best, usually found the answers. He could beat the cream of the golf world in head-to-head competition, but never finished in the money. He was accepted into the PGA in 1928 with the organization's highest ranking; however, his name never graced a PGA leaderboard, as it should have. Dewey Brown was black, banned from PGA competition. He knew that he could compete with the elite white golfers, and so did they, but Brown, despite his PGA card, the first issued to a black golfer, never got the chance.

Born in North Carolina in 1898, he moved with his family to New Jersey when he was three. He was hired as an eight-year-old caddy by the Madison (New Jersey) Golf Club and lugged bags and mowed fairways ten hours a day for a dollar. He also astonished members who saw him hitting balls in the gray hours just before dawn and at twilight, for he was nothing short of a prodigy, a boy who struck a ball farther and cleaner than most men. Later in his life, he said that he always knew that a golf course was the only place where he ever wanted to be. But the PGA had closed its events to blacks.

At sixteen, Brown applied for an apprenticeship at the tony Morris County Golf Club, having decided that if he could not play tournament golf, he could still work as an instructor. Brown was accepted, and began at the bottom by caddying for some of America's most famous financiers and their families. His cheerful smile and ability to hand experienced players the right club even before they knew it themselves caught the eye of club member John D. Rockefeller, who often picked Brown to caddy for him and began taking an interest in the teen. When the youth blurted that he wanted to learn the golf business and even hoped to save enough to buy his own club someday, the tycoon was so impressed that he insisted that the club's head professional, George Lowe, teach Brown how to give lessons, how to build and repair clubs, how to oversee maintenance of fairways and greens, and how to tackle all of the other myriad duties of a club professional.

Brown's friendship with John D. Rockefeller opened doors that the PGA and many clubs would have preferred to keep shut, and by the time that Brown was nineteen, he was certified as an assistant professional. Just married and about to start a family, Brown turned to Rockefeller for help in finding him a higher-paying assistant pro's job. The billionaire made a call that landed his ex-caddy a position at one of the nation's most exclusive golf resorts, the Buckwood Inn, in Pennsylvania.

A playground for millionaires, politicians, silent-film stars, and others among the Roaring Twenties' notables, the Buckwood offered Brown the opportunity to bank hefty tips from free-spending patrons, pick up stock tips, and establish a reputation as one of the game's skilled club-makers. Impeccably dressed in knickers and the latest in golf blazers, his hair stylishly parted in the middle and slicked down, he looked as sharp as his game. He was the most popular of the resort's assistant professionals, President Warren G. Harding insisting, whenever he visited the club, on a lesson and a round with him.

In 1928, Brown stunned the PGA by applying for full professional status, a Class A membership in the organization. Once again, he asked Rockefeller, as well as influential golfers he had tutored at the Buckwood Inn, for help. The PGA acceded to Brown's references and accepted him—but only as a club professional. The organization's 1916 whites-only clause quashed any of Brown's hopes that he could tee it up in PGA tournaments for cash against Hagen, Sarazen, Barnes, and other top-notch players. Brown always maintained that if given the chance, he would have won on the Tour; few who saw him swing a club contradicted him.

Although shut out of PGA locker rooms, Brown played on black golfers' answer to the whites-only PGA—the United Golf Association. Formed in 1926 by entrepreneur Robert H. Hawkins and inspired by the Negro Baseball Leagues, the UGA ran annual tournaments for black professionals and skilled amateurs alike. Brown, "Cross-handed" Howard Wheeler, Cliff Strickland, and other professionals banned from the big leagues because of the color of their skin battled each other in UGA events affectionately dubbed the "neckbone circuit."

The PGA had barred Brown from its tournaments, but could not stop his success in the golf business. In 1947, he drove to the

Adirondacks to view a piece of real estate, a small hotel nestled alongside Indian Lake. The rest of the property, however, interested him more, a nine-hole course in want of weeding, resodding, and new greens, but a scenic tract needing only a knowledgeable and patient course manager. For the reclamation project, he had just the right man—Dewey Brown had earned his Class A membership in the Golf Course Superintendents Association of America.

With money he had saved since his days at the Buckwood, Brown bought the Cedar River Golf Club in New York. The first black golfer in the PGA became the first of his race to have sole ownership of a club.

Over the next three decades, Brown turned his property into a thriving little resort, mowing the fairways, tamping down the greens as he had done as an eight-year-old caddy in New Jersey, overseeing every detail of his nine-hole lakeside gem. His clientele was mainly black, but over the years, many whites came to play the groomed little course again and again.

Aside from the course, the chief attraction of Cedar River was Brown himself, who served as head professional of his club until shortly before his death in 1973. A visitor to the course told *Golf Journal:* "A gentleman to the core, Dewey Brown is always dressed the part on the links. Look for the smooth swinger with the dark pants, mirror-shined shoes, white starched shirt with the tie and clasp matched with his always immaculate coat or sweater, and you have found this truly outstanding 'Knight of the Fairways.'"

Dewey Brown lived long enough to see Charley Sifford and Lee Elder win tournaments and respect on the PGA Tour. He had known John Shippen, the black golfer who had nearly won the 1896 U.S. Open and, in four other Opens, had at least tasted tournament golf against the best white players, and had proved himself their match. Racism had robbed Brown of the opportunity to compete, but not of a career in the golf business. Possessor of one of the century's slickest swings, teacher to many of the century's most powerful politicians and tycoons, club designer for PGA stars, owner of his own golf resort—these achievements would have been notable for any white golfer. For a black man in segregated America, they were nothing less than astonishing. Even more amazing was the PGA membership Dewey Brown wrested from the same officials who had decreed that their tournaments be as white as the ball.

A Family Affair

When a stocky, dark-haired golfer strolled into the Brackenridge Park clubhouse on February 1, 1931, few of the fans clotting the San Antonio course noticed him. Just two strokes off the lead and charging with one round of the Texas Open to go, he soon returned to the first tee, where only a small band of spectators greeted him.

While the name players, Horton Smith, Craig Wood, Ralph Guldahl, and others, had to wait for officials to settle the crowd before every shot, Abe Espinosa smiled and waved to his small knot of fans—most of them Mexican-Americans, as he was. Espinosa and his brother Al, also playing in the event, were used to galleries ignoring them at America's private golf enclaves. They were used to hostile stares from spectators and had learned to ignore comments about their ethnic background. They had learned that winning was the ultimate form of revenge against club officials who banned Hispanics from courses but were compelled to allow the Espinosas, card-carrying members of the PGA, on the premises.

Now, an Associated Press reporter wrote, Abe Espinosa, who had endured the stares and whispers in six previous Texas Opens and had come up empty in the event, "went quietly about his business of shooting two par-shattering rounds . . . and, not so quietly, ruined" his competitors' chances at the $1,500 prize. Rolling in long and short putts the entire round, he birdied the final three holes and waited for the rest of the field to finish.

When the scorecards were signed, the five thousand spectators who had followed other players realized suddenly that Abe Espinosa topped the leaderboard at two strokes over Tour great Joe Turnesa.

Espinosa accepted his winner's check, and in its account of the victory *The New York Times* described him as a "swarthy Spaniard." Once again, however, Abe Espinosa, the first Mexican-American to win a tour event, the 1928 Western Open, had proved that talent, not a golfer's surname, counted most on the course.

Before Lee Trevino, there were Mexican-American golfers Al Espinosa *(right),* and his brother Abe, stars of the Tour during the Thirties.

USGA

Abe Espinosa's younger brother Al, twelve strokes off the pace in the 1931 Texas Open, had also proved the point that Hispanics could play the game, and had even done so with more frequency than his trailblazing sibling, winning two PGA tournaments in 1928 and a grand total of nine, as well as earning a spot on two

Ryder Cup squads. Like three other Espinosa brothers who played on the Tour, Al and Abe had learned the game from the ground up as caddies at the Del Monte course, in Monterey, California, toting the bags of silent-screen stars, politicians, and industrial magnates. Each day the Espinosa boys showed up at the course several hours early, and they built games that their wealthy employers would never rival. When twilight came and the members headed to the clubhouse, the Espinosas played the course until nightfall chased them home.

By 1932, Al Espinosa had snagged a job as a pro at the Inglewood Golf Club, in Seattle, but was trying to play his way into the PGA's ranks. He first caught the golf world's notice with his victory in the Washington State Open, displaying a wonderful greenside touch honed in the fickle winds of the Monterey coast. He began playing in more PGA qualifiers, joined by his brother Abe, who, some professionals felt, possessed an even smoother putting stroke than his brother.

Abe's name appeared in sports-page headlines first. In the 1927 PGA, he battled through grueling match play to emerge in the final against Walter Hagen himself. The two put on a show for the throngs tracking them across Dallas's Cedar Crest Country Club, some fans reportedly hooting the Mexican-American between shots and quieting down only when Hagen glared at them.

To the crowd's shock, the twenty-three-year-old Espinosa led Hagen by a stroke as they teed off on the final hole, a tough par-four. Both players laid up their approach shots a bit, leaving Espinosa a twenty-five-foot putt for the victory. He rolled it way past the cup. Unnerved, he also pushed his second putt too far. He sank his third attempt to salvage a play-off, but his emotional focus was shattered, and Hagen beamed, heading toward the tee with his typical swagger.

Another three-putt debacle on the play-off hole completed Espinosa's nightmare. Hagen admitted to the Associated Press that luck had helped him win, but added: "What are you going to do? You give these guys a chance, and they don't take it."

Espinosa did not duck the press and, fighting back tears, stated that nerves had gotten the better of him and that he had fallen to "majors fever." Many reporters and PGA stars openly wondered if the young golfer could ever recover from the loss. A few even went so far as to hint that some nationalities did not have the right make-up to win on the tour.

In 1928, Al Espinosa shattered the "choke" label, if not ethnic slurs, by winning two Tour events. His brother Abe made even bigger news by seizing one of the Roaring Twenties' majors, the prestigious Western Open, at the North Shore Country Club, in Illinois. He became the first Hispanic golfer to win a big PGA event.

Of the Espinosa brothers, Al would earn fellow professionals' accolades as the best in his family and as one of the ten best professional golfers in America. He would win nine tournaments and earn a good living on the PGA circuit, but was viewed as a hard-luck golfer who fell just short in several majors.

Hard luck may have dogged Al Espinosa, but the hard work that he and his brothers never shied away from on their rise from caddies to their status as the PGA's first Mexican-American players was their true legacy. Their struggle foreshadowed the rise of another Mexican-American golfer three decades later—Lee Trevino.

East Meets West

The trio arrived in the United States to show off their expertise in "the universal language," the Associated Press proclaimed. Their language, however, was not that of Lothario or Casanova, but of the links. They were fluent in the "universal language that requires accurate shotmaking on the fairways and the greens." For the first time, Japanese golfers came to America to test their skills on the PGA circuit, but the players' names were not Aoki or Ozaka. Tomekichi Miyamoto, Rakuze Asami, and Kokichi Yasuda hit America's courses in November 1931, five decades before the former duo began to cash PGA checks with regularity in the 1980s.

PGA stalwarts Walter Hagen and Bobby Cruickshank already knew that Miyamoto, Asami, and Yasuda could compete with anyone on the course. In a tournament in Honolulu in 1929, Miyamoto had surged past the American and the Scotsman to lead the field after two rounds. But he had fallen apart in the final round, reporters claiming that the large, loud gallery had unnerved him. The claim rang specious, however, as Miyamoto had played calmly and well before throngs in Japan against "Wild Bill" Melhorn and Cruickshank, two of the PGA's finest shotmakers, who were spreading golf's gospel across Asia.

American newspapers jumped on the "East Meets West" theme of the Japanese players' arrival on America's courses, running such headlines as *The New York Times*'s "Japanese Golf Pros to Invade United States for First Time." Sportswriters noted that the trio were Japan's top players, Asami and Miyamoto Japanese Open champions and Yasuda his nation's perennial golfing runner-up with five second-place finishes in the tournament.

The three golfers arrived in San Francisco in late November 1931 and rushed off to the Lake Merced (California) Course, site of the Winter Tour's opening event, the National Match-Play Championship. Dozens of reporters tracked the Japanese golfers on their practice round to let readers know if the PGA regulars had anything to fear. In language that perpetuated a stereotype, a *New York Times* columnist wrote: "Three *smiling* Japanese smacked three amazingly long drives down the fairway of the Lake Merced course today, and the first golf professionals from the Orient to invade these shores had fired the opening shots toward an American campaign they hope will lead to some glory, some gold, and much experience."

The one who most startled observers was twenty-six-year-old

Kokichi Yasuda. They did not expect much distance as the five-foot-two-inch, 113-pound player addressed his first drive. Assumptions dissolved as he clouted a majestic blast down the first fairway and followed with one 275-yard tee shot after another.

All three golfers impressed observers. The Japanese "play methodically, almost mechanically," the *Times* related. "Each puts everything into his drive, with a tremendous swing. All putt alike, feet together, deliberate."

When asked by a wire-service reporter what they thought of American courses, one of the Japanese replied: "Much better than our own. Greens are better, faster. Ours [are] heavy, thicker grass."

A *Times* reporter's question about whether the Japanese players could win in America brought up the "stage fright" issue again. "We will try our best," the trio said. "We have not played before many large galleries."

The golfers spoke to the press through a translator about how much they liked America and asked the reporters a question: "Is Bobby Jones going to play in this tournament?"

The golfers were disappointed when told that Jones had retired from competition.

Although Yasuda, Miyamoto, and Asami never got the chance to tee off against their idol and did not win on the PGA winter circuit, they finished in the money in several events. They proved themselves to PGA players and afforded a flash of the future, in which Aoki, Ozaka, Vijay Singh, and other Asian golfers would assault the game's leaderboards.

Fighting Two Battles

He fit the image of the gifted golf professional, tanned and broad-shouldered. With his wide grin and neat, swept-back short hair, he should have been a popular figure at the country clubs of the 1930s and 1940s. He even had the game to match his looks. In the eyes of America's country club set, he had only one flaw, but it was a major one: Herman Barron was Jewish.

The son of hardworking middle-class parents, Barron had learned the game while caddying at the Fenway Golf Club, a Scarsdale, New York, preserve for mainly Jewish members. By the age of seventeen, he was a teaching professional at the club and was itching to test his burgeoning skills against the world's best players. But as a friend would recall, Barron would have to wage two battles— against the other golfers and against the anti-Semitism of blue blood country club officials.

Barron's booming drives and deft shotmaking were his weapons on the course, but in the clubhouse and in front of stone-faced galleries the only weapons he could use were self-restraint and a smile. If he lashed out at anti-Semitic remarks by anyone in the locker room, the PGA could ban him; if he erupted at club officials who had him seated in a dining room's worst table, far from those of fellow professionals, he could be barred from competing at the club ever again. Somehow, he controlled his emotions and answered by finishing in the money in nearly every tournament he entered in the 1930s.

Barron's game and low-key personality won him friendship from most of the players, but the feat he most craved, a win, eluded him time after time. He led several tourneys on the last day, only to see them slip away not because he choked, but because Craig Wood and other stars closed with miracle finishes.

In early February 1942, Barron and his wife, Carla, drove into the Phoenix Country Club for the prestigious Western Open, one of the nation's oldest tournaments. The course, long and fast, suited Barron's game, and his peers expected he would finish in the top ten, but few figured that he could end his thirteen-year Tour drought against the likes of Ben Hogan, Byron Nelson, and Sam Snead.

Not even after Barron seized the Open's lead after three great rounds was anyone willing to bet that he would win it. On February 8, 1942, a *New York Times* sportswriter marveled that Barron "utterly devoured the course and crushed the field" to finish with a "blazing 8-under 276." For the first time in American golf, a Jewish player had won an important tournament.

Barron received batches of messages from across the country, a handful of the messages vitriolic religious slurs, but most of them laudatory.

With the proverbial albatross lifted from his shoulders, Barron racked up other victories, the All-American Open among them, and he played on the 1947 Ryder Cup team. He had always answered the whispers and insults with his driver, irons, and putter. In 1942, they had proven his point that on the course, distance and a steady touch meant more than religious denomination.

"I'll See You in Court"

PGA president Horton Smith glared at the tall, slim black man who had entered Smith's San Diego hotel suite uninvited and unannounced on a morning in 1953. Smith, the winner of the 1934 and 1936 Masters, had carried one of his era's best games onto the course along with the prejudices of many whites. A traditionalist anchored to the "sanctity" of the PGA charter's Article Three—the 1916 whites-only clause—the wavy-haired Smith opposed the prospect of blacks entering Tour events, and the sight of PGA nemesis Bill Spiller further enraged the Missouri-born president.

If Smith wanted to call security to haul Spiller from the room, the PGA heavyweight suppressed the thought for good reason: seated near him was another heavyweight, boxing champ Joe Louis. "The Brown Bomber" had been invited to play as an amateur in the San Diego Open, and after Smith had banned him from the tourney,

Walter Winchell had harangued Smith and the PGA on a nation-wide radio broadcast and encouraged listeners to flood the organization's offices with telegrams of outrage.

Smith, compelled by fellow PGA officials to let Louis play, had relented and invited the boxer to discuss his participation's ground rules. But Bill Spiller, who had earned a spot in the tournament in a grueling Monday qualifier, had been told to clean out his locker and leave. When Spiller strode into the suite and demanded that blacks be allowed to play in any Tour event and that golf's ruling body drop Article Three, Smith said nothing, perhaps partly because Louis was in the room.

Spiller stared at Smith and the pair of PGA officials flanking their boss. No problem, Spiller said. They could discuss it with his lawyer. The golfer turned to leave the room.

Smith's aides shot from their chairs, rushed over to Spiller, and implored him to wait a day or two so that they could resolve the issues after the San Diego Open.

Spiller replied: "Sure, but if you don't, I'll see you in court."

Then, just before he walked out the door, he stared at Smith and the others. "You ran over me the last time," the golfer said. "But you aren't going to do that again."

Whatever else Horton Smith and the PGA of America's board thought of Spiller, they had learned that the determined thirty-eight-year-old golfer did not fear them or any other whites. The PGA of America had also discovered that Spiller, a college graduate, did not fight the game's whites-only policies on the course, but in the courtroom.

Enraged by the racism in the game, Bill Spiller wanted nothing more than a chance to play golf. As with countless players black or white, his apprenticeship came through various jobs at California clubs.

By his early thirties, Spiller had crafted one of the smoothest swings in the transient tournaments of the black circuit, the United

Golf Association, and, with the possible exception of Teddy Rhodes, had proved the purest ball-striker. Notwithstanding his self-effacing demeanor, Spiller acknowledged that he "won most of the tournaments in the black tour," but that unless he played Hogan, Snead, and the other Tour stars, he could not judge his game "against the best in the world." But he saw no way past the game's racial roadblock—Article Three.

In 1947, someone else, white golf lover and multimillionaire businessman George S. May, defied the infamous clause by inviting Joe Louis (as an amateur), Negro Women's Champion Anne Gregory, Teddy Rhodes, and Spiller to compete against the whites in the Tam O'Shanter Open. Run by May but tolerated by the PGA of America because he posted the game's largest purse, $50,000, and brought more publicity to the Tour with his "All-American" and "World Championship" competition than even the Masters did, May was the one tournament sponsor who could defy the Tour's ruling body and get away with it. When he invited Spiller, Rhodes, and company with the justification that an "open" tournament meant open to all races, the PGA of America acceded. The handful of black golfers who played in the Chicago event did not win, but they proved they could compete. Spiller, still near his links prime, walked from May's Tam O'Shanter Club convinced that, given the chance, he could someday win a Tour event, but only if he crashed the full tournament schedule. Always pragmatic, Spiller remarked: "You just can't go out and play against the best in the world with so little experience."

May's interpretation of the term "open event" encouraged Spiller and Rhodes to enter the qualifying event for the handful of available slots in the 1948 Los Angeles Open, and to the surprise of few Tour players who had seen both men play, Spiller and Rhodes seized spots in the tournament's field. They played well enough to cash modest checks from the sponsors. More important, because they had finished in the money, they claimed automatic entries into the Tour's next event, the Oakland Open, at the Richmond (California) Golf Club.

When Spiller, Rhodes, and black amateur Madison Gunter, the winner of the Open's Monday qualifier, showed up for the tournament, club officials assigned them lockers and caddies. Spiller and Rhodes played several practice rounds with PGA players Paul O'Leary and Smiley Quick, who greeted them with handshakes and smiles and bantered with them as they walked the course.

At the end of the sessions, Spiller and Rhodes returned to the clubhouse and found George Schneiter, head of the Tournament Players Bureau, waiting for them. In curt fashion, he ordered them to clean out their lockers and leave. The Oakland Open, he huffed, accepted regular PGA players only, and since neither Spiller nor Rhodes was a member, neither could tee off. Madison Gunter heard the same edict.

Rhodes, who was the same age as Spiller, shrugged, picked up his clubs and gear, and left. The "black Jack Nicklaus," as admirers later dubbed him, expected no more and no less from the PGA. He knew that, in his thirties, his best game had waned and so had any realistic chance for a PGA title. The younger man, however, was furious. Still he reined in his emotions, knowing that an eruption against Schneitzer would ruin any slim future hopes of a spot on the Tour.

From the Richmond Golf Club, Spiller headed for a phone booth and called an old friend who worked for a local newspaper. Johnny Merrins listened as Spiller, choking back tears, lashing out at the PGA, asked for help. Outraged at Schneiter's "eleventh-hour" tactic, Merrins said that he would make a few calls and persuaded Spiller not to leave town.

That evening, Ira Blue, a friend of Merrins and a sports producer for ABC Radio, broadcast Spiller and Rhodes's plight coast to coast, denouncing the PGA of America's underhanded ploy and branding its shifting interpretations of "open play" as not only unethical but illegal.

Spiller met next morning with reporters who had picked up the broadcast and would run diatribes against the last-minute ban against the three blacks, who had earned their place at Richmond by adhering to the tournament's own requirements. The PGA ignored the outburst, believing that the controversy would recede, as such flare-ups always had.

Golf's hierarchy could not ignore Spiller's next salvo, one that no black golfer had ever attempted. Years later, he said, "We decided we'd hit them where it counted." That site was a courtroom. Spiller had hired John Rowell, a black attorney who had just won a land-mark antidiscrimination suit against an Oakland housing complex, to challenge the Tour's whites-only dictates. A man whose name was already front-page news nationwide, Rowell could unnerve even the PGA of America.

The following day, Rowell hit the organization with a $250,000 lawsuit on behalf of Spiller, Rhodes, and Gunter, dismaying Horton Smith and several other Tour officials who sought a means of damage control while fashioning a loophole to gut the challenge. Several PGA of America attorneys chased after Rowell until they caught up with him on a train speeding to Los Angeles, where he intended to meet with the California attorney general to ratchet up the pressure on Smith.

The lawyers debated for hours, the defendant's team beseeching Rowell to drop the suit, which, they argued, would harm the very tour on which Spiller and Rhodes craved to play. Rowell retorted that the game's officials had only themselves to blame and that they would lose in court. Then, to Rowell's surprise, his adversaries offered their "guarantee"—Smith's official word—to cease all dis-crimination against black golfers and allow them to play in all "open" tournaments.

Bettmann Archive

Bill Spiller sued the Professional Golfers Association in 1948, eventually striking down the organization's "whites only" clause.

What about Article Three? Rowell asked. The PGA of America, the other lawyers said, would soon strike down the clause, but needed a few months to placate dissenters within the organization.

Believing that Smith and the other bureaucrats would not risk another public relations nightmare, Rowell shook hands on the deal and soon convinced Spiller and Rhodes that they could play on the Tour.

Within a few months, the black golfers discovered that the PGA of America had changed its tournaments from "opens" to "invitationals," and the only invitations issued by sponsors landed in white golfers' hands. Legally, if not ethically, the organization did not violate its pact with Rowell. Spiller and Rhodes went back to the UGA circuit, supplementing their incomes with caddying and other jobs. Rhodes was resigned to the situation, but Spiller bided his time, mulling ways to mount another strike against Article Three, counting on the PGA of America to slip up on legal ground.

In 1953, Spiller and Rhodes survived a qualifier for the San Diego Open, a "charity event" that Spiller had identified as "not under PGA auspices." Joe Louis had accepted an amateur invitation to the event, stacked with top-notch Tour players.

With so many circuit regulars in the field at San Diego, Horton Smith decided that the PGA of America did hold jurisdiction over the contest and dispatched officials to throw Spiller and Rhodes, as well as Louis, from the locker room. But then Walter Winchell went on the radio that same night and contended that if Joe Louis could carry a gun in the U.S. Army in World War II, he could carry a golf club in San Diego. Smith discovered through stacks of telegrams and phone messages that millions of white Americans supported Winchell's stance.

Enraged by the support for Louis, Smith nonetheless invited the heavyweight champ back into the tournament and arranged a hotel-room meeting to assuage the boxer's anger, but not to apologize to him. Using the word "amateur" as a public relations shield, Smith also summoned black golfer Euell Clark, who had made it through the qualifier, to the conference as "proof" that the PGA of America had barred Spiller and Rhodes only because they were not official Tour players.

Although many white players supported Article Three, the black golfers found a high-profile ally from the Tour. Jimmy Demaret, a colorful, sometimes profane player, the winner of three Masters and thirty-one PGA tournaments by his career's end, liked Spiller and Rhodes, respected their games, and believed that the PGA should open up the field for the best golfers of any color. Ben Hogan had said that if the high-living Demaret had practiced more, he could have won almost every tournament in which he played. Demaret's response to Hogan's comment had been to hoist a cocktail and toast: "I'll drink to that." His flamboyance aside, Demaret's opinion counted in Tour locker rooms, and he believed that Spiller should attend the conference in Smith's hotel suite, and called to tell him so. Spiller, who had not heard of the meeting, sped to the hotel and strode into Smith's rooms with an ultimatum: strike down Article Three and open up the PGA of America or try to defend "open versus invitational" in court. Then, Spiller demanded that the organization allow blacks to apply for head professional jobs on an equal footing with whites.

Although Smith refused to answer, two other PGA of America

officials pleaded for a "cooling-off period" before Spiller filed suit again. He smiled sardonically, staring at Smith, and warned them that they could have a few days, but would not "run over" him again.

This time, Spiller compelled the organization to amend its charter in writing: qualified black golfers were granted "approved entries" status to play in Tour events.

Spiller could wangle no more from the PGA of America at that juncture. By law, private clubs such as those hosting the bulk of golf tournaments held the right to appoint members and to invite guests as the sponsors wished. The clubs' "right of association" extended to golfers accorded the privilege of playing in club events, and with Smith and his cadre calling the shots for the Tour, Spiller harbored no illusions about his "victory." He remembered: "We had no voting rights in the [PGA of America], and the only tournaments we could play in were ones the sponsors invited us to. We got to play in Phoenix the week after San Diego, and the week after that in Tucson. In all, we got into five tournaments that year in the West, and five in the East."

Spiller showed up whenever he received an approved entry for Tour events, but, his game slipping a notch in his forties, he did not always make the cut against much younger players. "The best I ever did on the white tour was fourteenth in the Labatts Tournament, in Canada," said Spiller. "I got a small check."

Seven years after he defied Smith in the San Diego hotel, Spiller was supporting himself and his family largely through caddying at the Hillcrest (California) Country Club—a man who had competed against Demaret, Hogan, and other Tour titans carrying the bags of white weekend golfers. One day in 1960, new club member Harry Braverman was astonished to discover that his low-key, engaging caddy, Bill, was Bill Spiller, and asked him why he was not still on the Tour. Spiller responded that aside from his age, the PGA of America's invitation-only proviso closed too many tournaments to blacks, hampering their attempts to just earn a living on the links.

Braverman, urging Spiller to finish what he'd started, suggested that he write to Stanley Mosk, the California attorney general and a man sympathetic to the civil rights movement. Once again, the prospect of challenging the PGA of America prodded Spiller to act, and he penned a detailed missive about the thin legal veneer still masking the body's discrimination.

Mosk, a tenacious, clever prosecutor, met with Spiller and realized, as had Horton Smith, that the lanky golfer's pleasant smile and self-deprecating humor belied his passion for equality on the links. In just a few months, Mosk ramrodded legislation that held the PGA of America liable to civil damages for banning black golfers from any tournaments that operated on California's public courses. Mosk's law posed far more than a paper threat: on the 1961 Tour schedule, eight events worth over $1 million in winnings were hosted by public courses in California. And Mosk took his campaign nationwide, holding up Spiller as the classic case of a fine black golfer denied a livelihood as a bona fide professional. Mosk persuaded scores of other attorney generals to follow California's stance against on-course discrimination.

With legal pressure and the gathering surge of civil rights, the PGA of America pondered legal ploys to evade or at least stall Mosk's law, but the organization's attorneys concurred that the whites-only charter was doomed. The end officially came in November 1961 with the organization's announcement that, after forty-five years, Article Three no longer applied. The Tour, though not yet the minds of many players, lay open to blacks.

For Ted Rhodes, dying from kidney disease, "Cross-handed" Howard Wheeler, and other past stars of the "neckbone circuit," the victory over Article Three came too late. Charlie Sifford and, later, Calvin Peete, Jim Dent, Jim Thorpe, and Lee Elder endured hostile galleries and players and proved what John Shippen and Dewey Brown had known decades earlier: skin color made no difference in a golf swing.

For Bill Spiller, time's passage had also overtaken his game. Having opened the legal path to the PGA of America, he could only watch as the younger black golfers climbed their way up the leaderboards closed to him during his prime.

Spiller's legacy was not what he did on the Tour, but what he did *to* it in his victory over Article Three. Before his death in 1993, he saw Lee Elder take his place as the first black golfer in the Masters. In young Tiger Woods, Spiller glimpsed the game's future colossus. One can only imagine Bill Spiller's emotions had he lived to see Woods crush the field at the 1997 Masters, site of Horton Smith's greatest triumphs.

Zero Handicap

In 1931, twelve-year-old Ed Furgol dashed into a Utica, New York, playground with his friends, climbed onto a set of monkey bars, and leaped from one to the other. He missed the second bar, and his left elbow slammed into a cinder-block support, snapped, and tore through his skin.

Dazed, clutching his shattered left arm with his right hand, he stumbled from the playground as his friends surrounded him and cried for help. They flagged down a motorist, loaded their swooning friend into the backseat, and clambered in to accompany him to the hospital.

After several operations in just a two-week span to repair what a surgeon described as the worst compound arm fracture he had ever treated, Furgol's arm was imprisoned in a cast that held it over his head for six weeks. A caddie who already golfed better than the men whose bags he toted, and who dreamed of a PGA career, the boy prayed each day that his injury would heal. Until the cast was removed, the doctors said, there was no way to tell if he would ever have full use of his arm again.

Six weeks later, an orthopedist cut off the cumbersome plaster to find Furgol's arm locked over his head. They could not manipulate it past his shoulder for several more days, and when they finally lowered it, his elbow jutted at a forty-five-degree angle. The dislocation was permanent. They informed the boy that his hopes of a golf career had ended.

The doctors misgauged not only Furgol's obsession with the game, but also his willingness to endure physical agony to build a new swing. Every day, he spent two hours or more of excruciating stretching exercises designed to give him a modicum of flexibility. He still caddied after school and on weekends, building up his damaged arm's strength by hauling the heaviest golf bags he could find. When the last players left the course at dusk, Furgol hit countless balls, gritting his teeth as the pain surged through his arm. He admitted years later that each swing brought tears. But he refused to quit.

Slowly, Furgol developed a three-quarters swing that looked ungainly but worked. As he grew into a muscular young man, his added bulk compensated for the distance his crooked arm would have stolen from a slighter frame.

In 1939, the eighteen-year-old Furgol battled his way through tough competition to play in the USGA's Public Links Championship, a launching pad for teenage golfers who did not come from means but were chasing the dream of getting on the Tour. He did not win, but shot several of the tourney's lowest rounds, serving notice that despite his physical handicap, he had a high-caliber game.

By 1945, Furgol had reached the PGA ranks the hard way, through innumerable qualifying tournaments. Soon the Hogans and the Sneads did not even notice Furgol's disability—only his ability to challenge for the lead in virtually every PGA event, averaging a score of 71.4 in over one thousand professional rounds between 1945 and 1952. He rarely finished out of the money, his career an inspiration whether he ever won a major or not.

In the 1954 U.S. Open, at Baltusrol's Lower Course, Furgol played his usual form in the first two rounds, hovering within two strokes of the lead. He made his move on the third day, with unspectacular but steady play to a one-stroke lead over Dick Mayer and a three-shot advantage over the early leader, Gene Littler.

In newspapers' morning editions of June 19, 1954, sportswriters praised Furgol for overcoming his handicap and for inspiring other Americans to do the same. But the articles then prognosticated which golfer would surge from the pack bunched within five strokes of the lead to win the Open. Few believed that Ed Furgol's flawed swing could hold off the onslaught of smoother-swinging name players.

When Furgol and the rest of the field saw the tough pin placements and felt a tricky breeze sweeping the Lower Course, fans, reporters, and players accorded him even less chance to hold his lead, for the course would demand myriad swing adjustments that most golfers thought beyond Furgol's physical repertoire, through no fault of his own. Still, no one doubted his tenacity. And Furgol, mindful that he might never again come so close in a major, chose to play for pars and let the rest of the field worry about birdies.

With fifteen pars and two bogeys on the testing course, Furgol hung on to a one-stroke lead as he teed up his ball on the eighteenth. He scanned the par-five layout that curled in a slight dogleg to the left, lined by trees and a stream. If he drove to the left and kept it right of the trees, he could shorten his approach to the green and open up a chance for his round's first birdie, which would cement a victory. The safer play was to hit into the middle of the fairway.

With Gene Littler one stroke away from the lead, Furgol smashed his drive down the left side. The ball hugged the treeline for more than two hundred yards and suddenly veered into the woods.

Groans pealed from the gallery.

When Furgol reached his lie, the only shot he apparently had was to pitch back onto the fairway and leave himself two shots just to reach the green. He was staring at a bogey. If Littler held par, a play-off loomed; if Littler birdied, Furgol's gamble on the eighteenth would cost him the Open.

Agonizing over his lie, Furgol stepped back from his ball and looked at an opening in the trees farther left, where the

USGA

Ed Furgol, who overcame a crippled left arm to win the 1954 U.S. Open.

eighteenth fairway of the Upper Course stretched. He strolled over to the opening and saw that from the adjoining hole, he would have a clear shot at the eighteenth green of the Lower Course.

Furgol rushed over to a USGA official and asked if the Upper Course was in play or out of bounds for him. The official checked his rules book and replied that both courses were in bounds.

Furgol grabbed his eight-iron from his bag, scooped the ball from its brutal lie amid leaves and twigs, and angled his shot onto the Upper Course. Cheers engulfed him—he had an open path for a seven-iron to the green, the distance 150 yards or more.

The crack of Furgol's club against the ball signaled a solid swipe, but with no markers to refer to for such an unorthodox shot, Furgol had misjudged the yardage and came up five feet short of the eighteenth green, which had proved treacherous all day. Once again, the specter of a bogey materialized, especially since his putting had been the one shaky part of his game throughout the event.

Furgol nestled his chip shot five feet from the cup, but, he would say, the cup looked miles away. With his crooked arm, Furgol had a harder time drawing his putter back straight than most players, and his sometimes erratic stroke reflected that fact, not any bout of the "yips."

Furgol paused only for an instant, then curved his putt into the edge of the cup.

The gallery swarmed Furgol, his handsome features aglow with "that Major smile," the United Press reported. Sportswriters dubbed his victory everything from heartwarming and special to inspirational. Even on editorial pages reserved for weightier events than golf tournaments, columnists weighed in with acclaim for the man who had defied the doctors and had delivered his definitive answer to their pronouncements that he would never play golf for a living. That answer was U.S. Open champion Ed Furgol.

A Snowball's Chance

"Your daughter better win today, or you'd better not come back to this parking lot."

Carolyn Cudone's father had just been threatened by a parking attendant at the Meridian Hills Country Club, in Indianapolis, and knew why. Anyone who picked up a newspaper on September 17, 1956, understood: "A starting field of 105 players, including the first Negro in its history... was paired for match play in the 56th Women's Amateur."

In the opening round, Carolyn Cudone would play that "first Negro," Ann Gregory.

The hatred of many and the hopes of others swirled about Gregory, but, in the words of a supporter, the forty-four-year-old "was just the type we needed to break that barrier," the color line in women's golf.

Gregory was born in Aberdeen, Mississippi, on July 25, 1912, the child of Henry and Myra Moore, who worked for a wealthy white family named Sanders. When Ann was a teen, about the time she was fully beginning to understand the divisions between blacks and whites in small-town Mississippi, her parents both passed away. With relatives in the region, Ann's future did not point toward a "colored orphanage," and her parents' ex-employees, the Sanderses, soon "took in the girl!"

As Gregory would recall, the genteel family did not raise her as one of their own, an unthinkable scenario in Aberdeen of the era. They fed her, clothed her, and gave her a room; in exchange, she worked as the maid's helper and, in her late teens, "graduated" to the maid's slot herself.

In 1938, twenty-six-year-old Ann Moore, who had grown into "a handsome woman with great warmth," stunned the Sanderses with her announcement that she was going to marry Percy Gregory, a strapping, ambitious young man. Even more shocking to the Sanderses, who believed that their maid owed them lifetime service because they had rescued her from the orphanage, was her revelation that she and Percy were headed to Gary, Indiana, where he had landed a good-paying job at U.S. Steel, joining the migration of Southern blacks abandoning agricultural jobs for factories in the North.

"That family cried like babies," Ann Gregory remembered. "They said people in the North were so cold and that I didn't deserve being treated like that. I said, 'Mrs. Sanders, you've prepared me very well for mistreatment.'"

Gregory thanked the family for having provided her a job, walked from the house, and "never looked back."

In Gary, the newlyweds found a better lifestyle than in Aberdeen. They bought a comfortable home in a neighborhood full of other young black couples in which the husbands worked for U.S. Steel and the wives often worked in more "traditional" jobs—

as domestics and cafeteria workers. Gregory helped cater functions at local colleges and volunteered on church committees, the Community Chest, and United Fund drives. In an achievement that would have astonished both blacks and whites in Aberdeen, the all-white membership of the Gary Public Library Board appointed Gregory to the committee, making her the body's first black official and citing her intelligence and her popularity in the entire community.

Gregory not only devoted much of her time to causes and church, but also found a few hours each week to take up a pursuit closed to her in Aberdeen—tennis. A natural athlete in her teens, she discovered that her speed, strength, and superb hand-eye coordination were intact enough to put together a powerful serve-and-volley game that won her the Gary city tennis championship against several accomplished white players.

In 1943, "on a lark," Gregory joined the Chicago Women's Golf Association, an all-black organization with access to several public courses in the area. Never having picked up a club—"too busy with a mop all those years," she said—she took a few lessons from Calvin Ingram, a fine player who had won several UGA tournaments, the black golf circuit, but, like all black players, had been banned from the PGA of America. Ingram later said that he could hardly believe what he was seeing from her first swings—the best natural golfer he had ever coached.

Gregory, too, realized that she had stumbled upon an athletic gift, and with the same determination she brought to her civic concerns, she immersed herself in the game. Few golfers of any race ever built as good a game in just three years, let alone at the "over-the-hill" age—competitively speaking—of thirty-one. By 1947, Gregory had won the three best-known tournaments for black women golfers, the Chicago Women's Golf Association Championship, the Joe Louis Invitational, and the United Golf Association Championship. The black press anointed her "Queen of Negro Women's Golf," and mainstream white newspapers, including the *Chicago Tribune,* the *Detroit Free Press,* and *The New York Times,* began to notice her, speculating that her game might stand up to those of "white, fresh-faced, athletic young women who vied for silver cups on a tour of private clubs and resorts."

The directors of women's amateur tournaments from Palm Beach to Colorado Springs ignored the Queen of Negro Women's Golf, but a Midwesterner who had carved a fortune in retailing and was obsessed with gathering all of the best golfers, amateurs and professionals, followed the Gary woman's rising reputation.

In September 1947, the phone rang in the Gregorys' home, and Ann picked it up to hear George May inviting her to play at the Tam O'Shanter Country Club, in Chicago. He offered her the chance to play in his famed All-American Open against the nation's best female amateurs, all of them white.

When Gregory, concerned about how white players and fans would react, balked, May, whose panache and persistence had lifted him from door-to-door Bible salesman to mercantile magnate and earned him comparison as a pitchman to P. T. Barnum, convinced her that he did not intend using her as a "token" or to shock the white golf world. His tournament, he insisted, was for the best players, and he believed that she was one of them. Unless she played against white competition, he went on, she might never know just how good she was.

For several years, Gregory had told other Chicago Women's Golf Association members that she yearned to play in white events, and May's words tweaked her pride. Her own competitiveness pushed her toward accepting the offer. May's next words convinced her: "Mr. May told me if anyone said anything to me [at the tourney] to let him know." May's implied threat to handle any racism thrown her way at *his* tournament, at *his* club, sold her.

In the last week of September 1947, Gregory and her husband drove to the Tam O'Shanter for the week-long tourney, and for the first six days they saw no other black faces. As she played that week, however, she found that May had delivered on his promise to head off any racism. "The galleries were just beautiful to me," she said.

Later acknowledging that her nerves hampered her throughout play, Gregory shot scores that left her in the middle of the pack, not a threat to win the event. Several articles in black newspapers mused that if she had gone into the final round with a chance at victory, she might have found the galleries something other than "beautiful."

On the tournament's last day, Gregory, having said to her husband that for a whole week they had not seen any other blacks, walked from the clubhouse to the first tee, stopped short, and grinned. "My neighbors drove up from Gary to see me play the final round, and when I saw them, that's the only time I felt funny. It just did something to me to see my black friends among all those white people, and I cried."

There were rumors that several players had said nothing about Gregory's presence on the course but complained to tournament officials about the sudden appearance of her Gary supporters, and that May had told the complainers to play or leave.

Although Gregory had finished down on the leaderboard, she had won a victory by simply showing up for the event. Having encountered the white players' games firsthand, she conceded that their years of training had given them a competitive edge and that she would have to practice to close the gap. She gave every spare hour to the practice tee, hoping for an opportunity to play in a "real" women's event, one sponsored by the USGA.

In 1956, Gregory's chance arrived with the USGA's announcement that the amateur game's governing body had accepted the Chicago Women's Golf Association into its ranks. As the reigning champion of black women's golf, Ann Gregory could apply for a spot in all USGA tournaments, which included the most prestigious, the U.S. Women's Amateur Open. She immediately sent in her entry for that year's Amateur, and in the third week of July, she packed her clubs in her car, picked up her friend Jolyn Robichaux, and headed to Meridian Hills Country Club, in Indianapolis.

When they arrived, they found Joe Dey, the executive director of the USGA, "very eager to do everything that he could to see that her participation was pleasant." Gregory never referred to overt racism swirling around her at the club, but her friend Robichaux hinted at it: "We were so excited about the idea of her being in the championship that we didn't notice any problems." More important than the excitement, Robichaux, Dey, and Gregory herself concurred, she could handle the pressure: "Ann was the type we needed to break that barrier."

To Gregory's relief, she heard no epithets from the other players, who treated her politely, if not warmly in some cases. Golf historian Rhonda Glenn surmises that the other players' "backgrounds, so different from Ann Gregory's humble origins, worked in her favor." "If they were somewhat sheltered," Ms. Glenn writes, "they were also sporting and polite, and she would never hear hostile comments from another player."

The gallery and club officials and workers proved the chief sources of any muttered threats, catcalls, and ugly epithets hurled her way at the tournament. As she teed off with Carolyn Cudone, an outstanding New Jersey player and a Curtis Cup veteran, a huge gallery of spectators and reporters stood just feet away, all of them realizing that history was unfolding, many seething at the milestone that the round represented. Cudone's father smiled at his daughter and looked at Gregory, who happened to meet his eyes for a moment. He nodded and smiled at her, too. He had heard the parking attendant's threat—"Your daughter better win today"— just a few minutes before.

The announcer introduced Carolyn Cudone to a deafening burst of cheers from the crowd. A minute or so later, a thin smattering of applause greeted Gregory.

"Every reporter was there," Cudone would say. "You couldn't stir them with a stick! She must have been nervous as a wet hen, because as we left the tee, she said that if she didn't count her strokes right, it wasn't on purpose."

Gregory not only faced surly spectators and her nerves about her game holding up, but also carried another burden: in the days before the tournament, she had received stacks of telegrams ranging from good-luck wishes to warnings that she not embarrass her race by poor play. She also received warnings of a different sort—threats to pull out or else.

Gregory answered those threats with her first drive, a solid shot down the middle. And as she and Cudone focused on their match, both trying to ignore the roars that Cudone's best shots evoked and the muted claps that followed Gregory's strokes, racists' nightmares began to materialize. Cudone was playing solidly, but Gregory was racking up brilliant recoveries from bunkers and rough traps. On the back nine, she forged a two-up lead, a landmark victory just a few holes away.

A powerful woman whose long drives set up her entire game, Gregory suddenly began spraying her tee shots off the fairway. Some observers would claim that her nerve deserted her, but she had displayed more resolve than any other player on the field simply by showing up at the first tee. More objective and knowledgeable viewers attributed her sudden woes to aggressiveness: she wanted the match so badly that she overhit her drives, sacrificing control for more distance.

With each erratic tee shot and each misguided long iron meant to compensate for the first mistake, Gregory's lead dwindled. Finally, on the eighteenth, Cudone sank a pressure putt to eke out the win, two-and-one.

As the gallery erupted for Cudone, she and Gregory shook hands. Gregory leaned forward. "My husband said I didn't have a snowball's chance in hell," she said to Cudone. "I guess I fooled him."

Gregory, her taste for USGA competition whetted by her debut in the Amateur, returned for the 1957 Open, at Del Paso Country Club, in Sacramento, California, where she received another warm welcome from Dey, who would continue as one of her biggest boosters. A year earlier, she had made history merely by playing a round; in 1958, she entered the USGA record books with two match-play wins—the first ones by an African-American in an official event.

Gregory's foray into the 1959 U.S. Amateur was even more controversial than her 1956 debut. To play in the 1959 Open, at Congressional Country Club, in Bethesda, Maryland, she passed on an all-black tournament in Washington, D.C., infuriating the event's promoters and the black press.

At Congressional, Gregory received the usual heartfelt greeting from Joe Dey and a snub from Congressional's members. While dressing for the elegant pre-tournament dinner held by the Amateur's host club, she heard a knock on her hotel-room door and opened it to find an ashen-faced Dey. He told her that the club had banned her from the gala. He was powerless to do anything, he said, because the USGA had no control by law over any private club's social events.

In an interview years later, Gregory said: "I told Joe Dey it was no big deal. I said, 'I realize the money I paid to enter the tournament didn't buy stock in the clubhouse. I'll eat a hamburger and be just as happy as a lark, waiting on tee number one.' I didn't feel bad. I didn't. I just wanted to play golf. So I got . . . a hamburger and went to bed."

Over the next two days, Gregory went to work on her match-play opponents, especially her second-round foe, Georgia state champion Mrs. Curtis Jordan, the stylish, refined darling of the vocal gallery. Jordan snatched the lead on the first hole, and late in the match held a solid two-up advantage, club members in the crowd urging her to knock Gregory off "their course."

A handful of fans found themselves drawn to the underdog, and among them was PGA notable Frank Stranahan, a British Open and Masters runner-up and winner of the 1958 Los Angeles Open. On the seventeenth, Gregory tied the match, and a reporter noticed a nervous quiet in the gallery.

Both players planned their tee shots into the fairway, and

Gregory faced a tough three-iron across a pond to get on the green. She chose not to lay up, but to go for the pin. The slightest hesitation once she started her swing could splash her ball into the water. For Stranahan and other spectators good enough at the game to realize what guts it took to aim for the green, Gregory's choice engendered deep respect. Whether she could carry the ball over the water was another matter.

Gregory's three-iron smashed against the ball, a sharp crack echoing above the fairway, and sailed toward the water in a low arc—too low, some fans thought. The ball started to nose-dive halfway across the pond and for an instant seemed to have no chance to clear the bank, but it caught the edge and slid a few feet onto the green. Even those rooting against Gregory applauded.

Jordan, her face tight as she swung, flew her tee shot into a deep bunker. She followed with a wedge that left her with a long, twisting putt just to hold par. Jordan pulled it short; Gregory knew that a two-putt would win the match. She did not want to push her first putt too far, adrenaline taking over and leaving her a makeable but nerve-racking putt of a few feet.

"I stroked my putt, turned my head away, and heard the ball fall into the cup," she said. "All of the people began to applaud for once. When I made that deuce to win, my caddie turned a somersault. The club fired him for that."

Gregory dropped her third-round match, but was invited by Congressional's president to play the course anytime she wanted. "I thought, 'He's got to be crazy!'" she remembered. "I would never come back to play after all of the things they put me through."

A year later, she showed up in Tulsa for the Amateur, and a hotel manager refused to honor her reservation. She found a "black hotel" that had no air conditioners, and spent much of the night eating ice cream on the building's steps with her husband to cool off from the sweltering heat.

Gregory had proved her point that she could compete with white female golfers, many on their way to fame in the professional ranks. Then, in the early 1960s, she may have made her strongest point of all. In her hometown, Gary, the best public course was Gleason Park, which featured a well-groomed eighteen-hole layout for whites and a ragged nine-hole course for blacks. Gregory strolled into the clubhouse on a summer morning, handed the greens fee for the white course to the startled clerk, and informed him that because the nine-hole course held no challenge for her, she was going to play "the big course."

As she shouldered her clubs and walked toward the exit, she snapped: "My tax dollars are taking care of the big course, and there's no way you can bar me from it. Just send the police out to get me."

The police never came to haul her off the fairway. Hundreds of Gary's golf-loving blacks would follow her example, her action desegregating Gleason Park.

When Ann Gregory died in 1990 at the age of seventy-seven, she had proved right her old friend Jolyn Robichaux's prediction that she would "break down barriers."

"All We Need Is the Chance"

"You could back a million people up against the wall, white or black. Nobody would have gone through what I did—just to be a golfer." The speaker of those words would be compared to Jackie Robinson, with good reason. For the ordeals of Charlie Sifford ushered in the era of "open golf" for all races.

Charlie Sifford barnstormed the country in the 1940s on the UGA's "neckbone circuit," a rawboned slugger who could hit the long ball but lacked discipline around the greens. Teddy Rhodes, over a decade older than Sifford and a legendary player whom Ben Hogan called "one of the smoothest ball-strikers who ever lived," became Sifford's unofficial coach, mentor, and father figure and imbued him with the belief that he could play as well as any white.

"The PGA players don't hit the ball any better than we do," Rhodes said. "All we need is the chance to get in there and shoot with them."

As 1950 approached, Rhodes's athletic prime was slipping away, his game still solid, but no longer enough to beat the best young whites if given the chance. That chance was coming too late for Rhodes, but in his protégé, Sifford, the UGA's elder statesman saw the man who could "make the PGA nervous." From 1948 to 1954, Rhodes and several other top black players (see "I'll See You in Court") had battled the PGA of America in court to play Tour events, and Charlie Sifford became the beneficiary of the elder UGA stars' campaign when he and Rhodes received invitations to play in the Los Angeles Open. Despite surly galleries and several white players who refused to speak with them, Sifford and Rhodes finished in the money and hungry for more Tour purses.

Because of a hastily cobbled new PGA rule that only an invitation from tournament sponsors allowed golfers onto the fairway, Sifford received few opportunities to go head to head with the white players and continued to scrape a living on the UGA circuit, stringing together five consecutive National Negro Championships from 1952 to 1956. As he waited his next chance at PGA of America money, he practiced relentlessly. "I could smack a golf ball and make it go straight and far," he stated matter-of-factly. "And once I learned that, nothing was going to stop me from playing the game and getting better." To Sifford, "better" meant his name on top of a Tour leaderboard.

In November 1957, an invitation to the PGA's Long Beach Open sent Sifford on a cross-country drive to square off against such Tour "iron" as Billy Casper, Eric Monti, and Gene Littler. On the lush, long seaside course, $11,500 was up for grabs, a much larger purse than those Sifford chased on the UGA.

A few black reporters, as rare a sight at a PGA of America event as the golfers they covered, received press credentials at Long Beach, and when their lead stories for November 8–9 chronicled Sifford's "go for broke" strokes that positioned him only three shots behind coleaders Casper and Monti with one round left, blacks in urban areas and rural regions alike tuned in their radios for the latest sports updates. Sifford later said that he went to bed on November 9 thinking about heavyweight champion Joe Louis and Jackie Robinson.

The following morning, November 10, Sifford stepped from the clubhouse and marched up to the first tee, clamping a cigar between his lips and wearing a rakish brimmed hat, the picture of confidence. But his stomach churned as a gallery of five thousand congregated on the opening hole. Few of those faces smiled at him.

Eric Monti, a thirty-six-year-old Los Angeles professional whose chief claim to fame was his status as Hollywood stars' and starlets' instructor, was paired with Sifford for the final round. Sifford towered over the wiry, bespectacled Monti, who led the tournament because of his solid short game. Unlike several of the other players, Monti had conversed with Sifford several times, and just before they teed off in what Sifford later termed one of the crucial moments of his career, Monti nudged him and whispered a few words. Sifford grinned and then slammed a drive "right down the pike."

By the time Sifford and Monti reached the eighteenth tee, they and five other players had a chance to win. Monti nailed a tough putt to assure him at least a spot in a play-off, and Sifford approached his ball with ten feet left to the cup. Unless he sank it for a birdie, he was out of the tournament. As the gallery grew silent, he paced around the ball and squatted down several times to read the green, unable to use Monti's holed putt as a guideline because the position had been on the green's opposite side.

Sifford finally stepped up to his ball, reminding himself not to "choke the club," vowing not to leave the ball short and allow any- one to charge that he had been "too chicken" to take a run at the cup. He drew back his putter slowly, just as Teddy Rhodes had preached, and tapped it straight into the cup. As polite applause drifted around Sifford, Monti strolled up to him and shook his hand.

Both men returned to the clubhouse and waited for Al Besselink, Jay Hebert, Billy Casper, Howie Johnson, and Dale Anderson, all with "a chance to tie with Monti and Sifford by sinking reasonably short putts on the last hole." Each man missed his putt and the play-off. No matter what happened on the sudden-death holes, Sifford could finish no worse than second and could claim the loftiest finish by a black golfer in a white field: John Shippen's fifth-place notch in the 1896 U.S. Open had been the high-water mark. But Sifford entertained no thoughts of the runner-up slot. To him it seemed like taking second place in a fight—no matter the effort, he would still be the loser.

On the first play-off hole, a par-four, Sifford was on the green in two, but missed a birdie putt from twelve feet. He "breathed again" when Monti struck a ten-footer just wide.

Sifford's dreams plummeted on the second play-off hole when Monti fired a long approach shot within two feet of the pin. All that he had to do was to tap in his putt for the match. Sifford forced himself to watch, to "take it like a man and give that crowd no more satisfaction than they deserved." Monti's putt "lipped out," and Sifford had one more chance.

The third hole, a par-five, favored the long-hitting Sifford, and he held nothing back on his drive, walloping it nearly three hundred yards, nearly sixty more than Monti. Two strokes later, Sifford's ball nestled six feet from the hole, Monti's nearly twenty. Monti putted first and came up short.

Sifford later recalled that he blocked out the crowd, his nerves, Monti, the stakes, everything except the ball and the six feet leading to the hole and to victory. For that instant, he said, winning and beating a good player no matter what his color were all that mattered to him.

Sifford bent into his stance, cigar firmly in place, and "canned a six-foot putt" in front of the stunned gallery to become "the first Negro to win a major professional golf tournament."

In clubhouses of black golf courses throughout America, tears and toasts lauded Charlie Sifford. He pocketed the $1,200 winner's check and $500 more for the lowest round, 64, of the tournament, the largest payday of his career at that point. More important, however, to Sifford than the money and even his sense of personal vindication was his conviction that he had struck a blow for all the great "neckbone circuit" players barred from any chance to play against the best white golfers. He dedicated his triumph to "Cross-handed" Howard Wheeler and Teddy Rhodes.

Charlie Sifford, the first African-American to win a Tour event, the 1957 Long Beach Open.

USGA

Sifford's feat notwithstanding, the Long Beach Open champion's battle for a permanent spot on the Tour was far from over; the officials at Augusta quickly unveiled a new clause that effectively banned Sifford and any black who won a Tour event from the Masters. He refused to give up his quest for equality on the leaderboard.

For the next three years, Sifford racked up mileage on America's highways as he divided his time between UGA tournaments and the few PGA of America events to which he could wangle invitations. He finished in the money in every one, and in 1960, the PGA of America, responding to increasing pressure from the burgeoning civil rights movement and to the spate of court decisions against segregation, issued "player status" to Sifford.

Free to play in more—but not all—PGA of America open tournaments, Sifford "defiantly strode restricted fairways for others to follow." In April 1961, he made one of the more courageous athletic stands for equality by entering the Greater Greensboro Open, in North Carolina, where he became the first black to enter a tournament at a whites-only Southern country club. Death threats poured in by phone, telegram, and letter, and local police warned Sifford that they could not ensure his safety if he played.

Having stood up "in the face of harassment, discrimination, and physical threats," Sifford played the Greensboro Open, enduring four days of muttered expletives, "the silent treatment" from club members, and fans who cheered only on-course miscues he made. He did not win, but he did finish in the money, a moment he judged one of his greatest victories.

Every PGA of America tournament posed another test for Sifford, not only competitively, but also personally. Like Jackie Robinson in the late 1940s, the golfer had to restrain his temper despite blatant baiting by racists. Sifford knew that if he ever snapped and went after a venomous player or fan, he would be banned and that other black golfers might find their odds longer in pursuit of a Tour card.

"I was just strong enough to fight 'em and stay out here with 'em," Sifford reflected. "My attitude was give me a rock and a nail, and I'll beat you at your own game."

In his mid-forties, Charlie Sifford still beat them at their own game, winning the 1967 Los Angeles Open. He was still cashing checks on the Senior Tour in his seventies.

Sifford had helped to open the long-closed fairways of the PGA of America to Lee Elder, Calvin Peete, Jim Thorpe, and Jim Dent, Elder becoming the first of his race to play at Augusta.

"All we need is the chance," Sifford's mentor, Teddy Rhodes, had said.

Charlie Sifford's struggle gave black golfers that chance.

5

A Better Mousetrap

Fit to a Tee

On his way to work each morning and on his way home at night in 1899, a middle-aged man would step on and off a Boston street-car and pause outside Franklin Park Golf Course. He peered at golfers bending on one knee at the first hole, fashioning tiny, con-ical piles of dirt and carefully nestling balls atop the mounds. Then the golfers stood above their creations and drove their balls down the fairway.

The man who routinely halted outside the course had also built those diminutive dirt piles there—but only at sunrise or sunset. For despite his Harvard Dental School degree, the first awarded to an African-American, despite his well-cut suit, despite his gold pocket watch and chain, and despite the other trappings of his flourishing Boston practice, Dr. George F. Grant could only get on the course at off-hours. The reason was simple: he was black, banned from pri-vate clubs whose memberships he could afford, and relegated to playing behind white golfers on the public layout.

Despite his difficulties in getting on the course, Grant was obsessed not only with the game, but also with its physics, particularly those involved in lofting drives down fairways. And, like even the finest pros of the era, the dentist discovered the frustrations of driving off dirt mounds. No matter how flawless the swing, virtually every drive differed in height and length. Grant fingered those little piles of dirt as the culprit, and with the same craft and precision that he applied to fillings, the dentist worked on a solution to golfers' dilemma.

On December 12, 1899, after months of trial and error, Grant submitted an application to the U.S. Patent Office: "Be it known that I, George F. Grant, of Boston . . . have invented the Golf-Tee." His invention, a tiny wooden shaft with a tapered base and "a flexible tubular concave shoulder to hold the golf ball," was the world's first patented golf tee.

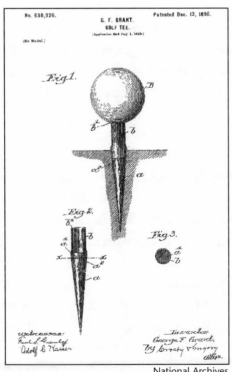

George F. Grant's patent drawings of the first golf tee, which revolutionized the game at the turn of the century.

National Archives

In stating his brainchild's simple purpose, the dentist sounded a revolution, literally raising the level of all golfers' games. "This invention has for its object," Grant wrote, "the production of a simple, cheap, and effective tee for use in the game of golf, obviating the use of the usual conical mounds of sand or similar material formed by the fingers of the player on which the ball is supported when driving off. . . . By the use of the tee . . . the player is sure that his ball is uniformly elevated from the ground at each drive, and the uncertainty of a sand [or dirt] tee is overcome, as it is practically impossible to make them of uniform height each time."

Although Grant had stolen a march on golf equipment designers with his milestone tee, the era's murky copyright infringement laws allowed entrepreneurs to copy the dentist's design and to market their own versions. Grant's tee soon showed up on courses on both sides of the Atlantic, but the profits did not flow to his bank account.

Twenty-two years later, in 1923, another dentist, Dr. William Lowell, an avid player at the Plainfield Country Club, in New Jersey, patented an improved wooden tee that was still strikingly similar to that of Grant. Lowell had discarded his first design, a gutta-percha tee that shattered too easily. When he carved one out of white birch, he found the answer to a cheap, functional tee.

Lowell's wooden tees, first painted green, then red, delighted his fellow club members, who dubbed them "Reddy Tees." Taking his idea to the professional ranks, Lowell persuaded Walter Hagen to blast balls off the Reddies, and, ever the promotional whiz, Hagen would intentionally leave them on the ground after each of his drives so that kids could grab them as souvenirs. Tournament officials became miffed by the scramble for Reddies and roped off not only tees, but also fairways and greens. A new form of on-course crowd control had materialized because of the Reddy.

With Hagen hawking the virtues of the dentist's durable tee, its popularity spread from America to Britain and to Japan, winning converts from professionals to beginners. The wooden-peg tee sold everywhere, but Dr. Lowell did not cash in. When he had filed his patent application, he had employed a friend and family lawyer who was unversed in patent law. The attorney left so many loopholes in the documents that by 1926, several hundred interlopers were marketing wooden-peg tees.

Today, whenever golfers tee it up, they owe two forgotten dentists, George F. Grant and William Lowell, a debt of gratitude. Their simple but savvy little inventions brought neither much money, but did forever end centuries of sand tees.

Bauxite Brassies

"Beware of spurious & unscrupulous imitations!" Readers could hardly miss the bold headline running in advertisements in newspapers in 1900. The warning referred to state-of-the-art, high-ticket items sold by the Bridgeport Gun Company, but not the outfit's usual lethal hardware. To a growing segment of readers, the admonition was riveting—after all, golfers did not want to pay top dollar for counterfeit aluminum clubs.

An aluminum plate was fixed across the face of the clubhead, with the "sweet spot" outlined. Ads promised that the clubs, patented by Mills' Standard Golf Company, would "improve your game" and were "backed by leading players" who were never named. Only if the club bore the stamped Mills logo on the aluminum plate was it "genuine."

The company offered every turn-of-the-century club—driver, brassie, spoon, cleek, driving iron, midiron, lofter, mashie, niblick, and putter—for the same price, nearly $40. At that cost, only the well-heeled golfer of 1900 could afford aluminum clubs, but, for a few years they proved popular. Most golfers, however, worried less about having bought counterfeit bauxite clubs than about adjusting to their lightness. Soon players reached again for their old brass-plated weapons, another "revolution" in club design fizzling. The search for an improved club and higher profits through technology, however, would never ebb, genuine innovations and their "spurious & unscrupulous imitations" a pricey and perpetual fixture of the game.

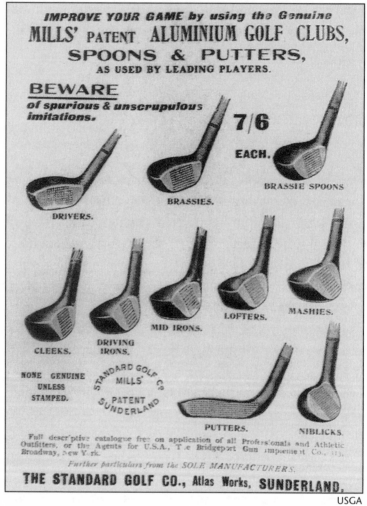

USGA

A 1908 advertisement for state-of-the-art clubs that had aluminum plates on their striking surfaces.

The Man of Steel

Few turn-of-the-century amateur golfers played a better game than Arthur Franklin Knight. And no American golfer knew more about golf clubs than Knight, whose radical new designs for drivers, irons, and putters forever changed the way the sport was played.

Clad in his well-tailored tweeds, with his well-trimmed mustache and sideburns and his short, neatly cropped silver hair, Arthur F. Knight fit the image of the successful scientist and engineer. His specialties were physics and engineering, but his passion was golf. A resident of Schenectady, New York, he took up the game during America's first golf boom, in the 1890s, he and his wife joining several private clubs. He approached a golf course with the same relentless study and deep curiosity that he brought to a laboratory.

By 1900, the fiftyish Knight had honed his game into one of upstate New York's finest, practicing or playing several hours daily. Never a man to downplay his achievements, he referred to himself as an "expert player."

As an expert in physics too, Knight pondered the basic forces that governed the swing from start to finish, always seeking the smooth, even flow of energy that produced a perfect stroke. As did even the best players of any era, he sometimes struggled with his swing's feel and wondered how his clubs could betray him when he was certain that his stroke was grooved. Knowing that the natural forces behind the swing were immutable, Knight became obsessed with the game's man-made instruments, the clubs. In his home's study, he pored over tomes on torsion, weights, and metals and wrote letters to club designers in Scotland and England. On the course, he would lay down a club after good or errant strokes alike, pull a small notebook from his jacket pocket, and scribble observations and diagrams. His research led him to the controversial proposition that a golfer's greatest foe was neither the course nor even his or her nerves, but the erratic properties of the clubs.

To put his theory to the test, Knight started with the game's smallest weapon, the putter. He spent months of study and experimentation in his lab at home, cutting and polishing hickory shafts and drawing up detailed blueprints for iron clubheads that a local foundry crafted for him. He varied the shaft lengths and the head size and curve, testing the strange-looking putters in his backyard, the click of iron against new dimpled Haskell balls marking his preoccupation at all hours.

In 1902, Knight walked into the office of a golf crony, the attorney Robert Read, toting something that at first glance looked like an elongated croquet mallet with a metal head. Knight handed the club to the lawyer and told him that he was holding the world's "perfect putter"—the center-shafted, mallet-style putter.

Other putters of the day were weighted at the point where the head's inside edge met the bottom of the wooden shaft. Since most golfers played the ball from the middle to outer edge of the blade, Knight had affixed the shaft to the middle of the blade, giving the club a natural pendulumlike motion and a center of gravity at the exact point of impact. The result, he told Read as the two filled out a three-page patent application and diagram, was a firmer, more manageable touch around the greens.

In 1903, Knight was awarded exclusive patent rights to the center-shafted putter, and he soon began to market his invention throughout the Northeast by sending test models to private clubs and by running advertisements in newspapers and in the widely circulated *Golfers Magazine.* He could barely keep up with the demand and by early 1904 was devoting most of his time to his fledgling club-making concern as the nation's golfers fell in love with the oddly configured putter.

Not all of the reviews of Knight's putter were laudatory. Many purists abhorred it, especially when some golfers used it to hammer putts with a croquet-style stroke, straddling the ball rather than setting up over it.

Critics notwithstanding, Knight's "Schenectady Mallet" made money from the start, and in 1904, one of the game's greats sent sales soaring. Walter Travis, who had won three U.S. Amateurs, was in England for a run at the British Amateur, but was mired in an agonizing slump with his putter. During a practice round for the tourney, he sprayed putts all over the rugged greens, cursing and tossing his club several times. An onlooker named Phillips winced at Travis's ordeal and gingerly approached him with a suggestion: why not try a Schenectady Mallet? A member of the Apawamis Club, in Rye, New York, and a devotee of Knight's invention, Phillips, a businessman who always traveled with his clubs, offered to lend his Schenectady to Travis.

Travis, who had heard of the putter but had never seen one, figured anything was worth a try, and Phillips dashed back to his course-side hotel, grabbed the putter, and raced back with it to Travis. He examined the odd contours of the club, hefting it from several angles, rolling it around in his hands. He then tossed several balls onto the green and set up over one, clamping a cigar between his lips and squinting through his round wire spectacles down the mallet's length. He rammed the putt home and soon holed others from all over the greens.

Travis went on to seize the British Amateur by dominating match play with putts from every conceivable distance and angle with his Schenectady Mallet. Knight's club had helped Travis to become the first American to win the prestigious tournament, and Travis helped Knight's reputation as America's preeminent club designer.

Travis's triumph sent shock through British golfing circles and also something else—a frenzied demand for mallet putters. At St. Andrews and other bastions of golfing tradition, clubmakers scrambled to turn out center-shafted putters, unhampered by any infringement concerns because American golf patents were not protected in the United Kingdom. Unfortunately for the club-makers, the R&A also refused to recognize the mallet as a legitimate putter, imposing a ban that dried up British markets before the new clubs even left the shop. The ban lasted until 1952.

Back in the United States, the USGA, elated that "one of ours" had snagged the British Amateur, tolerated the Schenectady as a legitimate, though unorthodox, addition to any player's arsenal. Nearly a century after the furor, Knight's center-shafted design would remain the prototype for countless putters.

Arthur Knight could have counted his profits and spent most of his time on the course. Actually, he did show up at local clubs nearly every day, but not just to play a round. He was formulating an even more radical change in club design than the center-shafted putter. Once again, he had fixed his scientific scrutiny upon the shaft, but this time with the intent to change the shaft's very nature by questioning whether hickory, the time-tested shaft material of all clubs of the era, was the most effective material. Knight's goal was as laudable to the golfer as it was potentially lucrative to the inventor: "to provide a practically torsionless club with which the player may make his game far more uniform and with which even a beginner may easily learn to play fair golf."

Knight's growing conviction was that hickory shafts' suppleness, which did increase distance, also robbed a stroke of the stiffness needed "to improve the fidelity of stroke." He based his theory on his own hands-on experience, noting the sole weakness of his accomplished game: erratic drives. "In driving," he wrote in a patent application, "I attribute . . . a lack of uniform quality in my playing" to hickory. While praising the wood's "hardness, toughness, and suppleness," he raised his "inherent objection . . . namely, the wood being fibrous in nature offers but small resistance to torsional strain and it therefore results that when the blow is delivered to the ball, the head of the club [twists offline] and causes the ball to deviate from the direction of impact."

In plain English, Knight's meaning was that the hickory shaft's sheer torsion forced a loose clubhead. "Unless the player by long training and practice unconsciously through experience has acquired a standing position to offset this inherent fault of the club, his play will be uncertain and irregular," Knight pronounced.

Having identified the structural enemy of consistent impact, Knight literally went back to his drawing board, as well as to the course. In late March 1909, he entered Robert Read's office with four clubs in hand. Read saw nothing unusual about them for a moment, as the leather grips and iron heads were still standard. Then the attorney's hands closed around the shafts, and moments later he reached for a blank application for "Specification of Letters Patent."

"To all whom it may concern," the lawyer wrote for his client. "Be it known that I, Arthur F. Knight, a citizen of the United States, residing at Schenectady...have invented certain new and useful Improvements in Golf-Clubs...."

"I have therefore dispensed with a fibrous shaft [hickory] and provided a practically torsionless construction....After much study and experimentation, I have finally been able to produce a club in which the necessary suppleness of shaft for a long drive and a true flight of the ball are both assured."

In the application's next line, a technological revolution for golf loomed: "I accomplish this by making the shaft of *steel tubing.*"

Knight's marriage of steel to the club's traditional configurations produced "a shaft so light and so rigid that it is not twisted by the hardest blow, and yet offers any desired amount of suppleness to suit the taste of the player and may be arranged to afford this suppleness at any point in the shaft length." Again, in laymen's terms, Knight was not only replacing traditional hickory with modern steel, but also opening the era of customized shafts. Eventually, his brainstorm would make pro shop owners a small fortune in woods and irons for players whose games were not special, but whose clubs could be.

On November 22, 1910, the Patent Office approved Knight's seamless steel clubs. However, the inventor's vision of golf's future came two decades too soon to profit him much. He died long before steel-shafted clubs caught on across America, in the late 1920s. The metal clubs gave American players such an advantage in length and touch over their Scottish and English counterparts that the R&A, still opposed to the Schenectady Mallet, legalized the use of Schenectady steelies for British golfers.

The technological revolution unleashed by Knight blazes hotter than ever in the 1990s. Titanium, graphite, and nickel-cadmium have won over many golfers, but many others remain loyal to supple steel, Arthur F. Knight's legacy to the game.

Four for the Price of One

Lining up a putt has tormented hackers and stars since Scots began spraying balls from Lowlands to Highlands. The task has proved tough enough when striking the ball with a putter's sole hitting sur-

Jeff Ellis

face, but in 1904, New Jersey-based golfer William Davis put an entirely new face on putts—actually, four faces. He adapted Arthur Knight's center-shafted design to a quad-putter whose head was

Four ways to torment oneself: the four-sided putter of William Davis, developed in 1904.

designed for ambidextrous players. The club permitted anyone missing putts with a traditional side-to-side swipe of the head to blow "gimmies" with a straight-ahead, croquet-style lunge with the club's toe or heel.

America's turn-of-the-century golfers delivered a quick verdict on the expensive Davis putter: four choices, none of them good.

The Weed-Whacker

In 1905, men thrashed through high, thick patches of grass on America's golf courses with a brand-new rake. But its seven iron teeth were open at the top, not the bottom, making the clubhead look like an inverted rake and failed to do anything except skim the grass and flatten it down, just as the instrument's inventor had intended. James Ross Brown had not patented a rake for groundskeepers and caddies, but a rake-iron for golfers whose balls lay buried in grass and brush.

An avid player who too often cursed traditional irons whose closed blades could barely dent dense grass, let alone reach a ball in it, Brown reportedly had his brainstorm while raking leaves in his yard. Noting how smoothly the tool's teeth skimmed through the grass, he reasoned that a golf club with inverted teeth would force the grass down and the buried ball up.

In 1905, he patented the rake-iron, which, he explained, actually raked the ball from the rough. For a year or two, his specialty club sold well, but it eventually lost its popularity because of three flaws—two a design problem, the other a matter beyond Brown's repair. His club did force balls from the rough, but they often slid backward from the open teeth, only to get airborne and nestle back in the deep grass farther from the fairway than the initial lie. The second design flaw was purely visual. Many golfers who loved the concept of a club that would part the grass to rescue trapped balls took a hard look at the rake-iron's toothy face and recoiled for aesthetic reasons. In traditionalists' eyes, Brown's invention looked too little like a golf club and too much like a laborer's tool, the very notion dooming the device at country clubs.

Jeff Ellis

James Ross Brown's rake-iron, 1905.

By the time that the USGA decreed that rakes belonged only in sand traps or in groundskeepers' hands, most players who had bought the rake-iron had already tossed it into sheds where it lay among shovels, spades, manual lawnmowers, and other yard tools. Occasionally, golfer/gardeners were spotted using the Brown Rake-Iron as a weeding tool.

Putting on Blinders

In 1916, a handful of American golfers put on blinders. Actually, they wore "blinkers," an Englishman's invention that purported to keep a player's eye on the task by reducing his or her field of vision to a small, square area around the ball.

As a fashion statement, the cumbersome glasses, with protruding lenses that narrowed like the tip of an ice cream cone, thrilled few wearers. But in 1916 or any following year, amateur golfers were willing to forgo fashion sense and comfort for fewer strokes on their cards.

Those who donned C. T. Ramsay's blinkers would ignore playing partners' stares and jibes, but only if the device worked. It did—sort of. Ramsay's brainstorm did force a player to keep his eye on the ball, because if he moved his head at all, blurred vision and dizziness followed. The only cup Ramsay's blinkers helped golfers find was the nearest trash bucket.

Positive Reinforcement

Hackers' fragile psyches crave positive feedback from club professionals. But in 1942, praise came from an unlikely source—a golf club itself. Whenever a golfer swung this club correctly, it "applauded."

The brainchild of Minnesota duffer George Carney, the applauding club featured a toothed roller affixed to the bottom of the head. He had placed the steel teeth to rub against a small brass plate attached to a spring.

A golfer would set up on the practice tee, in his backyard, or even in his garage or cellar with Carney's club, a five-iron. Then he would start his takeaway. If he dragged the clubhead for roughly sixteen inches before lifting it, the club applauded him for a proper backswing. The applause was actually a grating buzz as the roller rolled, the teeth contacted the plate, and the plate vibrated.

In his patent papers, Carney asserted that his club "would automatically cause the golfer to go into the correct pivot" for a sound swing. Unless the golfer dragged the club the proper sixteen inches, silence and a flawed swing followed.

For a short run after he patented his club, Carney made and marketed it himself, hoping to sign a pact with Wilson or another golf equipment titan. Several companies expressed interest and brought Carney in for a product demo. In the end, however, they passed because the club's applause was simply too annoying.

Let There Be Light

On a November 1927 night, a white arc of light illuminated the sky above Van Cortlandt Park Golf Course. Neighbors and fellow New Yorkers passing by peered at the strange glowing trail that looked, a World War I veteran told *The New York Times,* like "a slow-moving tracer bullet."

A crowd tracked the ebbing trail to the first tee, where an angular man stood with a driver. At his feet lay a small pile of aluminum-swathed golf balls.

Neighbors were used to seeing Millard J. Bloomer tee off at the course, but few knew he had been experimenting with an invention that he believed would revolutionize the game. To the *Times* reporter, Bloomer asserted: "I believe we will have all-night golf in a short time due to the luminous ball."

As the onlookers that November night stared at Bloomer, he reached down for one of the tiny aluminum packages, unwrapped it, and nestled its content—a ball glowing greenish yellow—on the tee. He set up over the ball and belted it down the fairway, and a phosphorescent trail once again lit up the sky. Then the ball dove back to the course and halted, pulsating with color. Even in the pitch black, no one could miss the ball, "shining in the fairway like a giant glowworm."

One by one, Bloomer emptied the pile onto the fairway, until several dozen balls gleamed like tiny beacons. Each ball's glow dwindled and died eight to ten minutes after Bloomer hit it. Even the slowest-footed golfers could home in on the ball during its minutes of life.

In another interview with the *Times,* Bloomer said that he and a Columbia University chemist whose identity the golfer refused to reveal had coated the balls with a "secret formula" and were working to refine "the substance that will produce a more permanent glow, like that of the radium composition used in watches."

Bloomer predicted that the glowing balls would open up every course in the nation to night golf. Left unsaid was his conviction that Wilson, Spalding, and other golf ball giants of the twenties would battle to hand him a fortune for exclusive marketing rights to his creation. There was just one problem: in trials of the ball, the "secret ingredient" spooked target customers, whose unspecified fears prompted sports equipment companies to drop the illuminated ball in a hurry. Unfortunately for Bloomer and his chemist friend, the adage "All that glitters is not gold" applied to their invention.

A Puff of Smoke

In 1928, Samuel Bens smacked a drive intentionally into deep rough and waited for his ball to thud to a stop in the brush. Suddenly a small silvery-white cloud wafted from the rough. Ben's ball had passed its scientific trial, and he rushed off to fill out a patent application to safeguard his secret formula—just the right amount of ammonium chloride to coat the ball and send a vapor cloud hovering above its hiding place. He had invented, so he claimed, an unlosable ball.

Bens, a New York chemist and golf buff, long tired of losing balls in off-course wilds, had decided to do something about his disappearing shots. After several months of trial and error spent smearing golf balls with various combustible compounds, he settled upon a relatively safe mix of ammonium chloride. Once his field test proved that unless the ball plunked into water a player could not lose it, Bens marketed his invention with dreams of wealth. Golfers were impressed by the ball's smoky signature, but recoiled at the pungent smell it left.

Undismayed, Bens returned to the lab for a new approach to finding golf balls, a trial by fire, or, more accurately, by firecracker. He purchased a batch of spit devil, a highly flammable compound used in Fourth of July pyrotechnics.

Bens dipped a ball in the volatile stuff, reminding himself that a little would go a long way. What he had no way to gauge as he teed up his creation was if even a little was too much. If his calculations were wrong, his experiment could blow up in his face.

His own guinea pig, Bens swung the club. There was a short, sharp explosion as the clubhead crashed into the ball. It sailed some distance, and as soon as it hit the ground, a series of small explosions pealed long enough for Bens to chase the ball and follow the noises to its resting place. To his delight, Ben found the ball intact.

The experiment's success notwithstanding, Bens soon discovered that while many golfers loved the idea of their shots literally exploding, club officials were not willing to have their courses echoing like small war zones. Golfers would have to find their errant shots the old-fashioned way: by thrashing around in woods and rough.

The Eyes Have It

In 1932, General Electric built a machine that was a revelation. The device measured the speed and the power not of amps and current, but of a golf swing. The "Electric Eye" looked decidedly low-tech to the untrained observer. A golfer stepped atop a wooden platform and lined up his club to a ball teed up on an adjacent wooden platform. To the right of the tee, a speedometer and a photoelectric eye were hooked up to time the speed of the club as it struck the ball.

Bettmann Archive

Long-drive champion Jim Reynolds tests General Electric's Electric Eye, built in 1932 to measure swing speed.

General Electric's first guinea pig for the device was Jim Reynolds, a fine professional golfer and a former national long-drive champion. He stepped onto the platform in the company's Schenectady, New York, laboratory and took a swing too fast for the small crowd of scientists to follow from takeaway to impact.

The blurry motion of Reynold's swing was not too quick for the contraption. With a slight hum of wires the only sound except the crack of club against ball, the electric eye measured Reynold's swing at 125 miles per hour. Less excited by the speed of Reynold's swing than by the machine's ability to read it, the scientists broke into applause—for each other.

At the 1939 New York World's Fair, the electric eye attracted millions of visitors who climbed onto the platform to see how their swing measured up against America's best golfers. The results, of course, were predictable.

Like baseball's radar guns that measure the speed of a pitch, golf's electric eye would stick around in "new and improved" versions. Myriad devices that measure the speed, or lack of it, in golfers' swings would flourish on practice tees, in pro shops, and in golf equipment outlets.

Man and Machine

William Beil and Floyd Farley, a pair of physics teachers, patented the perfect swing. Not their own swings, but that of their revolutionary machine. In 1943, the two Oklahoma City golf lovers and inventors constructed a steel contraption with an "arm" jutting downward and outward and clenching a five-iron just below the grip. All a golfer—and prospective buyer, the duo hoped—had to do was stand behind the arm, set up in his golf stance, grip the club, and uncoil his usual backswing.

At first for most of the inventors' golfing guinea pigs, the club and its metallic arm would not budge, no matter how they strained. Baffled, they asked the inventors themselves to set up behind the machine and swing the club fluidly. They did it easily. The test cases demanded to know the machine's trick.

Beil and Farley revealed their secret: the metal arm would lock whenever a golfer's movements violated the proper swing plane. From backswing to follow-through, the machine compelled the golfer to learn the correct club positions.

A 1950s swing aid.

The Ralph W. Miller Golf Library

The correct-swing machine did not make its creators wealthy men, but did earn a profit. Golf clubs, instructors, and a handful of wealthy players were the only ones who could or would pay the device's $150 price. The heavy machine, however, proved one of the first practical swing trainers.

Nearly six centuries later, the countless stroke savers endorsed by Greg Norman, John Daly, and other name pros tally enormous profits. Two Midwestern golf buffs whose names no modern golf entrepreneur would recall pointed the way with their modest metal arm.

Atomic Golf

Within a B. F. Goodrich rubber core, a secret ingredient ticked— plutonium. The device was not an A-bomb, but a golf ball that required a Geiger counter.

In June 1950 at the Portage Country Club, in Akron, Ohio, B. F. Goodrich engineers introduced the golf world to the "Talking Ball," whose voice was one-fiftieth of a gram of plutonium that would make an approaching Geiger counter crackle. Company officials reassured players that the ball's radioactivity posed less threat to them than a common X-ray.

The bizarre by-product of the Atomic Era was designed to end one of the weekend golfer's chief laments, lost balls. By switching on a hand-held Geiger counter after swatting the radioactive ball, a golfer could track it, the machine's "beeps" growing louder the closer a player got to the ball and its atomic core.

The combination of plutonium and Geiger counter worked— but feebly. The ball's radioactivity had to be low to be safe, and the weak emissions did not register on the machine until a golfer stood within four feet of the ball.

Sales of the ball proved as wan as its signal. Perhaps, in an era when the Red Scare filled American's collective nightmares with mushroom clouds, any idea featuring radioactivity on the fairway was doomed to fail.

All the Right Moves

As a golfer stood in front of the swing aid in 1953, he probably gulped. He might be willing to try anything to smooth out his swing, but this apparatus looked like some relic of the Spanish Inquisition. Even the device's name grated: the Anti–False Move Machine.

The golfer's dedication to improving his game was really put to the challenge. The machine's operator strapped the player's feet to foot plates. Then the attendant grabbed a leather cap and chin strap dangling from the machine's scaffold-like crossbeam and fixed them on the golfer's head.

After a truss linked to the machine by three metal rods was yanked around his waist, the golfer obeyed the order to grab a club that was anchored like a sailboat's boom to the frame. He was about to *feel* the flaws in his swing.

Isolating and correcting flaws from setup to follow-through had driven George Jenks, the machine's inventor, to the drawing board. A Florida scientist who had broken down every element of the proper swing and had translated each movement from paper to pulleys and metal, Jenks based his elaborate creation on a simple idea: a golfer could feel the way that a swing should unfurl if his head and body were keyed into the proper positions.

Once a golfer was strapped into and bound by Jenks's hardware, the machine did all the work. It automatically forced the club and the golfer's body to work in unison, the cap keeping the head on the ball, the truss controlling the hips, the foot plates moving slightly and compelling the knees and feet to obey the dictates of precise movement. The club's motion—set to the perfect swing plane—controlled the golfer's wrists, elbows, and shoulders.

Jenks's machine worked, forcing one to feel the correct swing again and again, tapping into what sports medicine would label "muscle memory." But the device contained a few bugs. Not only did the straps and belts chafe and pinch, but the machine's perfect settings did not mesh well with imperfect body types. Those who buckled up for a ride on the Anti–False Move Machine felt the perfect swing—and felt muscle pulls from the device's rigidity and headaches from the circulation-cutting cap and chin strap. Like so many other well-intentioned golf aids, Jenks's invention ended up on the game's technological scrap heap.

6

Helping the Hapless

The Father of American Golf?

In Burlington, Iowa, in 1883, a young golfer blasted his tee shot into the summer haze—and into local golfing lore. According to Iowan tradition, Thomas "Andy" Bell had not only become America's first homegrown golf pro, but had also done so on the first course in the United States.

Was a three-hole Burlington tract east of Madison Avenue truly the nation's first course? And was local boy Andy Bell the first American golf pro? Bell's and Burlington's claims run into the "twin towers" of early American golf—John Reid, dubbed "the Father of American Golf," and his three-hole course in a Yonkers, New York, cow pasture, named St. Andrew's.

Notwithstanding Reid's stature, Andy Bell made a strong case for the pair of golfing firsts. His Burlington friends and neighbors had no doubts about where the "cradle of American golf" lay and about who placed it there.

From his early years, much was given to and expected of Andy Bell, whose father, William, had proved the quintessential self-made man in Iowa business and political circles. Born in Scotland in 1818, the elder Bell had emigrated to Iowa as a young man and had carved out successful dry goods and grocery concerns that made him a key figure for the farmers of the county. Hard work and growing prosperity earned the merchant a cupola-topped mansion on Madison Avenue, and he and his wife, Marion, raised Andy and his two sisters in comfort, but imbued them with the virtues of honest labor.

Andy Bell grew into a popular young man in his hometown. Square-jawed, curly-haired, genial, and athletic, he did not coast through his youth as an indolent son of wealth but worked hard in and out of the classroom. Still, he did indulge one trait made possible by his family's wealth: a taste for stylish clothes. His friends dubbed him "Dude."

In Andy Bell's late teens, his father sent him off to Scotland's prestigious University of Edinburgh, not just to study, but to experience the heritage in which the senior Bell took so much pride. The Iowan discovered the classics at the university and something else, Scotland's collective pastime—golf. Throughout his sojourn, Bell laid aside books and papers whenever possible and scurried off to play eighteen. From Edinburgh's Bruntsfield Links to the most hallowed shrine of golf, windy, rain-swept St. Andrews, Bell embraced the game with the passion and touch of the born golfer.

In 1883, Bell came home to Burlington with a "kit" of hardware strange to most locals except Scots. Cleeks, brassies, niblicks, and white gutta-percha balls—they were the tools of the ancient game young Bell wanted to teach his friends and neighbors. And, proving to his father that business remained just as important to his heir, Andy Bell boasted that he had brought home his landmark clubs duty-free.

Dude Bell wasted little time hauling his clubs and gutta-percha balls to open acreage just down Madison Avenue from the Bells' manse. He measured and laid out a three-hole course.

Bell soon found plenty of company in his Madison Avenue meadow. He spread his golfing message and explained the timeless mysteries of the swing plane with equal patience for athletic or clumsy novices alike. His popular on-course sessions made Dude Bell America's first recorded pro.

By 1896, Bell's three-hole layout had evolved into a nine-hole course, which, the *Burlington Hawkeye* contended, "has the distinction of being the first golf club west of the Mississippi." He did not, however, abandon the family business for the links: in the 1890s, full-time professional golfers in America were considered no more than skilled tradesmen by upscale Americans. For Andy Bell, the family mercantile came first.

In 1912, Bell left Burlington to pursue family business interests in Chicago, where he became one of the area's top golf professionals. The golf fever that he had carried to Burlington spread even after his departure, several more clubs springing up around town in the 1920s.

Still dapper but no longer so robust, Bell visited his hometown in the late 1920s and was accorded a celebrity's welcome by the local press and golfers alike. "It's been nearly twenty years since I was in Burlington," he remarked to the local newspaper, "but I always consider it my old hometown. . . . What looks the best to me are the faces of old friends and the old landmarks and the old river that remind me of the past. . . . Oh, it does look good."

Burlington's golfing past and present merged when Andy Bell stepped up to the first tee of the Burlington Golf Club and lifted a drive down the familiar turf. "Mr. Bell was delighted with the Burlington course and pronounced it one of the best in the Mississippi Valley," the *Hawkeye* reported. "He should know. . . . 'Dude' Bell is known wherever golf is played as the man who brought golf to this country and laid out the first golf course in the western hemisphere, right here in Burlington."

In June 1932, less than three years after that triumphal round in Burlington, Andy Bell died of heart failure in Chicago. His family brought his body home to Iowa and interred him in Aspen

Grove Cemetery. His final resting place bordered the spot where he had carved out his three-hole course nearly fifty years earlier.

By the time of Bell's death, golf historians had entrenched John Reid as the Father of American Golf. The name of the man who had brought the game to Burlington five years before Reid hacked away across his Yonkers pasture slipped into golfing obscurity, although Bell himself had never been shy in touting himself as a golfing pioneer and claiming that he had introduced golf to the United States. His hometown supporters never wavered in their belief that Burlington had a case as the birthplace of modern American golf. "There has been a good deal of controversy about the first golf course," a *Hawkeye* article related, "but Mr. Bell let the others put in their claims and then proved, by documentary evidence, that in [1883] he returned from school in Scotland with a bag of golf clubs...and laid out a course east of Madison Avenue—the first in the United States."

John Reid or Andy Bell? Many Midwestern golfers had no doubt about *their* choice.

Loopers

In a meadow, two little boys shouldered their burdens manfully. They awaited orders from four men standing amid leafless trees and patches of snow. Directly in front of the group, a photographer set the exposure and took a landmark shot: America's first golf picture. And center stage in that image were not only four players with putters poised, but also those two little boys, the nation's first recorded caddies. Until the advent of golf carts, players who would never have dreamed of toting their own bags relied on the boys for hauling clubs all across the "loop," or course.

USGA

"Loopers." In America's first golf photo, taken in 1888, Harry Holbrook's sons lug clubs for their father, John Reid, and company at St. Andrew's Golf Club in Yonkers, New York.

The boys, dubbed "loopers," lugged the clubs of John Reid, Harry Holbrook, Kingman H. Putnam, and Henry Tallmadge across the rough turf of St. Andrew's Golf Club in Yonkers. Introducing the boys to the game and finding a way to spend some family "quality time" in nineteenth-century style, Harry Holbrook had drafted his two sons to carry their dad's and his cronies' clubs.

The pair proved willing walkers and really had to work for their wage. "No bags were used," one of the milestone caddies would recall, "and but one gutta ball was carried by each player. I think the name of the ball was Eclipse. They cost thirty-five cents each, and when one was lost, St. Andrew's Golf Club declared a moratorium until it was found. The clubs cost from $2 to $2.50 each. When one was broken, it was necessary to send to Scotland for the head or shaft, as the case might be."

A glimpse of the two caddies in the photo reveals that they had been lectured about the value of the clubs: the boys clutched them with two hands, balancing the men's mashies, niblicks, and brassies on small shoulders. Beneath his cap, one of the loopers stared at the camera with a focused, almost grim expression. Neither boy wanted to drop a club and risk his wages, a princely one to a youth of the era: twenty-five cents per round.

By 1910, youths from eight to eighteen dragged golfers' bags on private and public courses alike. Some of the youths were shorter and lighter than the bags they shouldered. At many swank courses, some captains of commerce and scions of old money treated the loopers, most of whom hailed from poor families, with disdain or ignored them altogether, except to bark out which club was desired. Caddies learned to keep their eyes lowered and their mouths shut, knowing that at country clubs, they were the lowest form of the help. Sometimes, a member ticked off after a poor round would stiff the looper, blaming him for not pulling clubs from the bag fast enough and upsetting the player's "rhythm." Small wonder that in various group photos of early caddies, few smiled.

In 1932, young caddies did catch a break of sorts. Several courts nationwide not only banned golfers from slapping or kicking their own caddies, but also held players liable if they harmed other golfers' loopers. After years of ducking irate hackers' blows, caddies' chief concern shifted from physical to verbal abuse. As anyone who has witnessed a PGA player erupting at a caddy who suggested the wrong club or misgauged the distance to a pin knows, the weight of words will always vie with the weight of the bag as the looper's chief lament.

"Knock Hell Out of It!"

The little boy felt the teacher's eyes on him. Those pale blue eyes, narrowed in the sun-beaten face, scrutinized the child's every move.

A youthful Bobby Jones displays the follow-through and finish of the "Carnoustie swing" taught him by Scottish professional Stewart Maiden.

USGA

A pipe clamped between his lips, the man snapped in a thick burr: "Square yourself around a bit."

The boy obeyed. The man still peered at him, the scents of tobacco and the man's tweed jacket suddenly closer.

"Move that right foot and shoulder back a bit," the man ordered.

Again, the boy did as he was told.

Several moments passed, the boy gritting his teeth, afraid to move. Finally, his limbs starting to ache, he murmured: "Now what do I do?"

The man replied: "Knock hell out of it!"

Six-year-old Robert T. Jones, Jr., swung as hard as he could and cracked a low drive straight down the middle of the East Lake Golf Club, just outside Atlanta.

That session, Bobby Jones recalled decades later, was his first real golf lesson.

Jones's instructor, Stewart Maiden, had said little more. He rarely did. For the fifty-year-old head professional of the club, words came sparingly and only when necessary. But the Scot knew his craft, gleaned amid the gorse and seaside gusts of his native Carnoustie, where he had mastered the "Carnoustie swing," a smooth, consistent arc with minimum joint stress.

Maiden had both a knack for spotting youthful talent and uncanny luck. He was already teaching a freckle-faced, redheaded twelve-year-old whose mastery of the Carnoustie swing far outshone that of any East Lake player except Maiden himself at the moment. Her name was Alexa Stirling, and her father, the British consul in Atlanta, and mother were Scots who shared Maiden's love of the game. Stirling, who would win three U.S. Women's Amateur Opens and many other tournaments, had embraced Maiden's minimalist message: stop talking, stop thinking, and "knock hell out of it." Now six-year-old Bobby Jones had heard it too.

Decades later, Harvey Penick's *Little Green Book* and *Little Red Book* preached the same sort of uncluttered message, though in a far folksier manner than Stewart Maiden's brusque credo.

Golfology

By 1930, golf's rising popularity had created a newfound respect for instructors. Once branded just another form of the help by affluent hackers, accorded only a little more appreciation than a gifted gardener or a skilled cook, tournament and club professionals were courted by socialites, Hollywood stars, and public course devotees alike.

Professional golfers welcomed the recognition that their craft was a bona fide vocation born of talent and practice. In a 1931 Associated Press article, Ernest Ryall, the head professional at the Forest Hills–Ricker course in Augusta, Georgia, gave an interview about the genesis of his trade from hired "grunt" to "top gun," drawing comparisons to the evolutions of two other professions. "Insisting that the introduction of modern science in the ancient game of golf has wrought developments at least equal to those through which undertakers have evolved into morticians and ditch diggers into excavators," the reporter noted, "Ernest Ryall . . . moves that golf teachers change their name. He suggests 'golfologist.'"

While holes in the ground figured prominently in all three professions, Ryall's fellow golfologists must have wished that he had discovered common ground somewhere other than a cemetery.

7

Who Needs Lessons?

One-Shot Wonder

John Pierpont Morgan took instructions from no one, or so his business foes and associates thought. But in 1897 at Shinnecock Hills, a small, sinewy young man was *telling* the famed financier how to do something—swing a golf club. Even more amazing to anyone who knew Morgan, hardly a social reformer, would have been the facts that his instructor was John Shippen, a black golf pro, and that Morgan was listening.

Although Morgan was nearly sixty, he towered over Shippen. The young professional could see that the tycoon, a burly man with huge shoulders, should be able to hit a golf ball a long way. Morgan's legendary self-confidence had sent him to Shinnecock with little doubt that he could master golf as he had America's financial game.

At Shinnecock, Shippen had learned from head professional Willie Dunn how to cater to the egos of captains of industry and still teach them the game. No prospective player, however, carried a more intimidating visage and demeanor to the practice tee.

According to *The New York Times,* Morgan's "eyes could be icy and his frown terrifying. . . . His manner at times was abrupt and dictatorial. . . . He dealt in ultimatums." His ultimatum to Shippen was blunt: teach the game to a man who did not think much of the sport and was wondering what the fuss was about among his golf-loving peers.

Shippen took Morgan through the mechanics of the swing, and after a few practice hacks by the tycoon, escorted him to Shinnecock's first hole, the Mews, shaped a conical tee out of sand, and perched a ball on it.

Morgan peered beneath his shaggy eyebrows at the pin, 275 yards away. If the hole's scenery could not seduce one into a lifetime passion for the game, nothing would: from the first tee stretched a vista of the windswept Sebonac Bluffs, Shinnecock Bay, and Atlantic whitecaps through which ships of all shapes and sizes passed.

Morgan also would have spied something else. Just seventy-five yards away, a windmill stood in the fairway. Countless duffers straining to loft their balls over the obstacle topped drives or sprayed them toward a nearby row of horse sheds.

Morgan took his stance, facing the windmill. The tycoon swung and cracked a drive that soared over the windmill, kept climbing, and landed on the green. Neither Shippen nor any other professional could hit a much better drive on the Mews.

Morgan did not head toward the green. He turned to Shippen, pronounced that golf offered no challenge, and went home. According to Shippen, J. P. Morgan never picked up a golf club again.

Swing from the Heels

Most American golfers had heard of the great Harold "Chip" Hilton, but until the 1911 U.S. Amateur Open, few had seen his unique game. Winner of the 1892 and 1897 British Opens and of the 1900, 1901, and 1911 British Amateurs, the forty-two-year-old legend arrived with his hickory clubs to play in the U.S. Amateur and to show the Yanks how it was done. He showed them how to win by defeating Fred Herreshoff in a thrilling play-off at the Apawamis Club, in Rye, New York, and by becoming the first golfer to bag the British and U.S. Amateurs in the same year; however, his style of play grabbed even more attention than his nail-biting victory.

By any golfer's reckoning, Hilton's swing and style were quirky. He played in white sneakers, a fashion faux pas that Rye officials ignored only because of his stature in the sport. His knickers and jacket looked as if he had slept in them, and he wore a battered little caddy's cap as far back on his crown as he could, another fashion affront to the leisured galleries at the 1911 Open. If anyone wanted to locate Hilton on the course, all he had to do was follow the trail of ashes from the fifty or so cigarettes he smoked per round. No one

Chip Hilton, amateur champion of Britain and the United States in 1911 despite a ragged swing and a cramped putting style.

USGA

could remember seeing him swing without a cigarette glowing between his lips.

If Hilton's unkempt appearance and chain-smoking were not enough to horrify golfing blue bloods, his swing would. To make up for his slight frame, Hilton heaved every ounce of his body into his drives, feet leaving the ground at impact, but somehow he managed to hit the ball clean and deep.

First-time observers of Hilton were slack-jawed at his wild but effective shots down the fairway and encountered another stylistic surprise once he reached the green. He grabbed for a putter that looked as though it belonged to a child or had been cut in half. Bending so far over the ball with his diminutive club that he nearly squatted, he soon showed America's golfing elite why he was acclaimed as one of the most lethal putters Britain had ever produced.

A 1990s golf equipment giant's ads urge players to "find your game." Harold Hilton had done just that—mastered a wild swing and a cramped putting style that allowed him to "win ugly." Although fellow professionals admired his triumphs, purists would always abhor his swing. No self-respecting golf tutor would have used Hilton as a model for students.

Diegeling

Anyone seeing Leo Diegel's putting stance for the first time gawked. His forearms hovered parallel to the ground, his wrists tight and straight as he clutched his putter against his chest. His posture, which could scarcely have seemed more awkward, looked more appropriate for one of the trick shots he was known for than for one of the pressure putts he faced on the PGA Tour of the 1920s and 1930s. Appearances notwithstanding, his ungainly style, dubbed "Diegeling" by fellow professionals, sank enough balls to net its sole practitioner twenty-nine Tour victories, including two PGA Championships.

Diegeling was a method born out of misery, Leo Diegel's incessant struggle to control his jittery on-course psyche. Like so many players of all generations, he suffered most on the green, battling what Sam Snead labeled "the yips."

In his natty fedora, the wiry, good-natured Diegel, one of the all-time great iron players, belied the image of a golfer struggling with his nerves. He became gregarious, sophisticated Walter Hagen's best

Leo Diegel, the 1920s star whose elbows-akimbo putting style was dubbed "Diegling" by his fellow players on the Tour.

USGA

friend, the pair forming golf's "odd couple"; although Hagen was a master needler capable of jarring other players' concentration and did just that to win several tight matches against Diegel, their bond endured.

Hagen, knowing that Diegel's nerve rarely faltered until he reached the green, reserved his jibes for moments when Diegel faced a critical putt. The tactic worked enough that Diegel experimented with countless stances to steady his hands and his nerves. He finally settled on the elbows-out, joint-tightening stance that became his trademark.

In the 1928 PGA Championship, at Five Farms Country Club, in Baltimore, Diegel and Hagen met early in the match-play format. Hagen was defending four straight PGA Championships. In a tight clash with his friend, he waited until Diegel stood over a four-foot putt on the thirty-fifth hole. If Diegel buried it, Hagen's streak was over.

Diegel gripped his putter against his chest and jutted out his elbows, his ball in front of his left foot. With Hagen's eyes fixed on him, Diegel buried the putt—and some of his inner demons. He went on to win not only the 1928 PGA, but also the next one, "Diegeling" every clutch putt.

Same Cup, Same Game

On August 24, 1932, Charles H. Calhoun, Jr., and two other golfers hugged his father, who had just aced the third hole of the Washington Golf Club, in Washington, Georgia. The elder Calhoun's hole in one was the first in the course's history.

After the excitement subsided, Calhoun Junior measured his own tee shot, a medium iron on the par-three, and lofted his ball at the pin. His shot landed a few feet from the flag, bounced twice, and vanished into the cup.

In a wire service blurb that ran in hundreds of newspapers and was picked up by radio networks, millions of golfers marveled at the Calhouns' milestone: no other father and son had ever aced the same hole on back-to-back shots.

The duo's hometown took a great deal of pride in the locals who had each made a "hole in one in the same cup and the same game." The club's members reveled as much in the Calhouns' feat as in Washington's other noteworthy feature: "This [Georgia] town, named for the immortal George [Washington] and believed to have been the first town in the United States so to honor the great American, makes another bid for recognition."

8

Grip It and Rip It

Far and Sure

At first glance, he looked like a bank clerk, not a legendary golfer. The members of St. Andrew's, in Yonkers, had paid the Scotsman's passage so that they could take swing lessons from him and pit him against other clubs' name Scottish pros—Shinnecock's Willie Dunn and The Country Club's Willie Campbell. When Willie Park, Jr., stepped off a transatlantic steamer in New York, his slight frame, neatly parted hair, and long, trimmed sideburns hardly fit the image of a man renowned for prodigious tee shots.

When Park walked into the little St. Andrew's clubhouse for the first time, any doubts among the members dissolved. He wore the blue-collared scarlet blazer of the fabled Musselburgh Golf Club, where eighteenth-century Scottish players had first codified the game's rules. He looked every bit a two-time winner of the British Open and the son of Open winner Willie Park, Sr. On his jacket's crest, the Musselburgh motto proclaimed skills that John Reid and his golf buddies were paying for: "Far and Sure."

Willie Park, Jr., the Scottish-born professional who awed Americans with a 248-yard drive in 1895.

Golf House

In late May 1895, several hundred spectators and a contingent of reporters clotted St. Andrew's to see if Park could deliver on the Musselburgh credo. Reid had arranged a match between Park and Willie Campbell, a clash that *The New York Times* would dub "the most important in many respects that has ever been played on this side of the water."

East Coast newspapers had touted the caliber of the players for weeks, lauding Park's short game and Campbell's consistency. But the handful of Americans who really knew the game wondered if Park, whose last triumph had been in the 1889 British Open, had begun to slip. In the past few years, his drives, always long but sometimes erratic, soared off-center more often, a sign that he was forcing his swing to cling to the yardage of his youth.

Park walked to the first tee at St. Andrew's with a more immediate problem than middle age encroaching on his swing. A giant boil had risen the previous night on his neck, and as he took a few practice swipes, pain surged through him. Only by cocking his head at an odd angle could he get full extension on his swing. The adjustment did nothing to ease his distress. Still, with his reputation and a winner-take-all purse of $100 at stake, Park never considered anything but playing his round.

Park's opponent was similarly handicapped by a physical problem. Campbell, whose game revolved around his subtle refinements of grip and touch, was suffering from an infection on his right hand, which was swollen to twice its normal size. He could barely close his hand around the club, but, like Park, he never considered bowing out. As one of Britain's noted players and the winner over Willie Dunn in America's first professional match, at Newport Country Club in 1893, Campbell had his own reputation to protect. As 1890s "working stiffs," professional golfers played if they could stand—and the nobs of St. Andrew's and Shinnecock were not inclined to listen to excuses from business employees or their club pros.

Park and Campbell did not disappoint, dazzling the crowd with cunning iron play and clever putts. The players' tee shots, however, most captivated the gallery and reporters in a nineteenth-century portent of twentieth-century Americans' obsession with distance, whether a tee shot, a home run, or a long bomb on the gridiron.

Although the newspapers praised the wide range of shots both players displayed in the match, won six and five by Park, writers devoted most of their accounts' space to a 248-yard drive that Park uncorked. *The New York Times* marveled at the stroke, "the longest drive ever recorded in American golf, the best . . . up to that time having been around 197 yards." Park himself had stomped around in disgust in the seconds after his ball landed: he had driven seventeen yards past the 231-yard hole. He scrambled to make his par-four.

Despite his distance, Willie Park, Jr., lived by the links adage "Drive for show, putt for dough." He proclaimed: "The man who can putt is a match for anyone." Park's game embodied not only that maxim but also the Musselburgh motto—"Far and Sure."

Of Ruthian Proportions

As he took a few practice cuts on a late August afternoon in 1929, a buzz rippled through onlookers. It did whenever the man swung.

He settled into his stance, eyes narrowing beneath his brimmed cap. He spread his spikes in the familiar pigeon-toed way that somehow balanced the surprisingly spindly legs and burly torso.

Staring at the white ball, he waited an instant. Suddenly his arms, wrists, and hips uncoiled, and the sharp crack of wood against ball brought a collective gasp from spectators. His swing always did.

The ball soared higher and farther against a cloudless blue sky, swinger and fans alike craning their necks. Finally, the ball plummeted, bounced a few times, and rolled to a stop 325 yards away.

Babe Ruth lines up at putt in 1927, the year he swatted sixty home runs.

USGA

Onlookers gaped. They had never seen a ball hit that far—not even by the shot's barrel-chested creator, *Babe Ruth*. This Ruthian clout, however, had not settled into the upper deck of Yankee Stadium. His drive had come down dead center in a fairway at St. Albans Golf Club, in New York.

In 1927, the Sultan of Swat had launched baseballs over major-league fences a record sixty times, routinely belting 400 to 450-foot shots. That no ballplayer had hit baseballs so far so often was a given in the game's circles. But in his glory days with the Bronx Bombers as part of "Murderers' Row" with Lou Gehrig and Tony Lazzeri, Ruth was also launching tee shots farther than anyone else in the Roaring Twenties. Not even Walter Hagen and other golf greats of the day could "airmail" it like the Babe.

Famed on the diamond for swinging a longer, heavier bat than fellow players, Ruth applied the same "bigger is better" approach on the links. He blasted golf balls with a custom-made oversized driver—his forty-five-inch-long, sixteen-ounce "Bludgeon." In pro-am matches, celebrity tournaments, and long-drive competitions, Ruth drove the ball farther than anyone. Gene Sarazen, Hagen, and other premier golfers who teed it up with Ruth could only stare as he outdrove them by a wide margin. Luckily for professionals whose egos might have urged them to swing harder in any ill-advised attempt to match Ruth's yardage, the deficiencies in the Bambino's short game outweighed even his distance on the scorecard.

The same confidence that had allegedly spurred Ruth to point to a spot in the bleachers during a World Series game and "call" his ensuing homer had led him to believe that he could drive any hole. He could not. At Bermuda's Mid-Ocean Club, he peered down the fifth, a 430-yard tract calling for a drive across a lake. A dogleg left teased the golfer to cut off large stretches of the lake. The more he cut off, the shorter his approach. Ruth believed that he could drive the entire lake. In a scene reminiscent of Kevin Costner's disastrous effort to clear the water hazard in the film *Tin Cup*, Ruth splashed eleven balls into the lake.

Ruth's brazen approach to the game, his Bludgeon, and his celebrity status as America's most famous athlete brought paying customers to any golf event in which he played. In his inimitable way, he helped bring golf into the big leagues of American sports in the tumultuous twenties. In his rakish Scally cap, which, to tweak nobs' noses at private country clubs, he wore backward, his cardigans, his knickers, and his natty two-toned spikes, the Sultan of Swat brought his great public appeal and his great distance, if not a great overall game, to the courses of the era. Throughout his life, he reaped many athletic honors, but one in which baseball's home-run icon particularly reveled was his 1932 presidency of the American Left-handers Golf Association.

Today, as golfers tee off with Big Bertha and other alloyed war-clubs that have mediocre weekend players launching drives 270-plus yards, one can only imagine the acreage Ruth's drives would have chewed up with a titanium or "bubble-burner" Bludgeon.

9

Misery Loves Company

Reversal of Fortune

"Who is that man?" The question rippled through the gallery following the slight, thirtyish golfer across New Jersey's Englewood Club in the opening round of the 1909 U.S. Open. His name was Dave Hunter, and on the sultry morning of June 24, he was taming the fast 6,200-yard course in a way no one ever had, and shaping a round that no Open golfer had ever matched. Spectators who had never seen the Essex Club professional strike a ball before gaped at his crisp drives, so startling from so diminutive a frame. But Hunter's putting was his real trademark: he nailed them long or short all morning. The rest of the field, including such stalwarts as Walter Travis, Willie Anderson, and Tom Vardon, a great player and brother of the greater player Harry Vardon, averaged thirty-six putts on the tricky Englewood layout. Hunter walked off the greens after thirty putts with a card of 68, the first player in Open history to break 70.

As the players filed into the elegant clubhouse for a breather before the afternoon round, Hunter's spectacular play and the swelling heat dominated conversations. The golfers guzzled water by the quart; some were already dizzy from the strong sun, Hunter among them.

When the players gathered on the clubhouse piazza for the second round, the heat swelled past one hundred, and dozens of spectators chose to sit on chaises beneath striped umbrellas rather than to follow the golfers across the steaming course.

As leader, Hunter teed off first, and within six holes, his once-crisp cap sodden with sweat, he seemed to wobble several times as he stood over his ball. His shoulders drooping noticeably, his magical morning touch on the greens vanished, and three-putts piled up for the Essex professional.

The heat also beat down many of Hunter's competitors as the mercury soared, and Hunter's score rose in unison with the thermometer. So severely did Tom Vardon feel the heat that he nearly withdrew from the second round.

When Hunter reeled onto the eighteenth late in the afternoon, his score stood at 79, eleven higher than his record morning round. A large crowd viewed his plight, for automobiles had deposited well-heeled spectators along a ridge flanking the final green. The *Times* reporter seemed less interested at the moment in Hunter's woes than in the crowd's many "young women, a pretty picture in their light summer frocks." Hunter saw nothing pretty as he bogeyed the final hole and lurched into the clubhouse to down more water.

In the course of a few searing hours, Dave Hunter had tumbled from the single best round in the Open's annals to thirteenth on the leaderboard, a turnaround of sixteen strokes. Hunter's plunge continued with scores in the eighties for the final two rounds, and he not only fell out of the money, but also garnered the dubious distinction of one of the Open's worst falls from grace—first to thirty-first.

The *Times* summed up Hunter's descent: "His Waterloo came in the afternoon."

Dave Hunter's putting touch abandoned him in competition after his 1909 debacle of Englewood. In several more U.S. Opens, he never came close to triumph or to his trailblazing sub-70 card.

Ill Winds

Ed "Porky" Oliver had tasted his share of hard luck and disappointment on the Tour in the 1940s and 1950s. A burly man who could crush a ball off the tee but also had a fine short game, he burst onto the Tour in 1940 with three wins and unofficial rookie-of-the-year status. Other professionals needled Oliver about his girth, but never his considerable game, one that many thought would win him a major or two.

In his first year on the Tour, Oliver nearly fulfilled that promise in the 1940 U.S. Open. He was tied with Gene Sarazen and Lawson Little after four rounds at the Canterbury Golf Club, outside Cleveland, but as he and five other players—Claude Harmon, Ky Laffoon, Leland Gibson, Dutch Harrison, and Johnny Bulla—had signed their third-round cards, the wind picked up, and a thunderstorm slowly gathered above Lake Erie and swept toward the course.

Scanning the dark clouds and guessing that they could get in their final round, Oliver and the other five rushed to the first tee and swatted their drives into the damp air. After the eighteenth hole, USGA officials ran up to both threesomes—Oliver was playing with Harrison and Bulla—and disqualified them for beginning their round ahead of their official tee time.

Five took the news stoically, as they were nowhere near the lead. Oliver, however, fought back tears, for his 287 would have put him in a play-off for the title against Sarazen and Little the next day. On a stool in front of a clubhouse locker, Oliver slouched, his head down, wiping his eyes. To a United Press scribe, the golfer mumbled:

"It's not just the honor of having a chance to win the Open. I need the money, and I need it badly."

The newspaperman understood: with the Depression still in full swing, most Americans needed the money. From all across the nation, fans understood Oliver's lament, too, and they besieged the USGA offices with letters and telegrams in support of the disconsolate golfer. Accusations of poor sportsmanship and dictatorial conduct by golf's ruling body filled the newspapers and the radio; several commentators advocated a purge of USGA officials. The organization held its ground, maintaining that the rules were the same for Oliver as for everyone else.

Oliver went on to play well in several other U.S. Opens, finishing second in 1952, but never won a major. Even after his retirement, the memory of his 1940 disqualification still galled him.

Oliver did win many PGA events. But in 1954, he encountered another misadventure that, along with the 1940 U.S. Open, would mar memories of an otherwise stellar career. In the opening round of the Bing Crosby Pro-Am in January 1954, Oliver teed up his ball on one of golf's most scenic holes, Cypress Point Golf Club's sixteenth, a 235-yard par-three that played like a par-four when the winds swept in from the Pacific. Clearing a stretch of the ocean to reach the green in one was a problem on such days, but Oliver, a long hitter, figured he could blast his tee shot through the gusts and right at the flag.

Several minutes later, Oliver stood on the green, but thirteen of his balls lay in the surf below the cliffs. When the shaken golfer tapped in his second putt, he carded a sixteen on the sixteenth. Spectators still shaking their heads at the sight of Oliver slamming balls into the surf and muttering and stomping around the tee only to plunk another into the Pacific had viewed a fine golfer who played himself out of contention by a bout of stubbornness. Over the years, that sixteenth hole would dare golfers of all abilities to go for the green, and the Pacific below would claim countless balls and ruin countless rounds.

Read 'Em and Weep

Fifteen-year-old Barnette Pung let out a whoop, dashed onto the eighteenth green of the Winged Foot Golf Club, in Mamaroneck, New York, and hugged her mother. Jackie Pung had just won the 1957 U.S. Women's Open, and as mother and daughter wept with elation, the gallery cheered, many fans also wiping their eyes. All that remained of the Open was for the victor to sign her card and collect her trophy and check.

Sportswriters covering the event did not always hit it off with professional golfers, but it was different with Pung. Perennially cheerful, never difficult or unkind, she was the most popular player on tour, and after she had fallen short in several major tournaments, the press had rooted her on as she battled the winds raking Winged Foot for three days and came up one stroke better at 298 than the estimable Betsy Rawls.

Jackie Pung shortly before her mistake on her scorecard cost her the 1957 U.S. Women's Open title.

USGA

Pung and her partner, Betty Jameson, signed their scorecards, and once again the Pungs embraced to the crowd's applause. No one noticed USGA officials suddenly huddled together and studying the twosome's scorecards, frowns on several faces, disbelief on others. One of the officials walked over to Pung and said something in a low voice. She gaped at him for several seconds and fought back tears—but for another reason than moments ago. She had added up her correct score, 72, but had mistakenly logged her fourth-hole six as a five; by USGA rules, if any player signed an incorrect scorecard—even if the total strokes were right—he or she must be immediately disqualified. Amazingly, Jameson had made the same mistake on her card and was also disqualified.

The mistake, utterly honest, stunned the gallery and the press, and, with Pung summoning enough composure to embrace the new winner, Betsy Rawls, as she accepted the $1,800 winner's check, the crowd sympathized with the Hawaiian golfer. Many sportswriters on the scene recalled her grace and smile after her play-off loss to Rawls on the 1953 Open.

Linc Werden, a *New York Times* golf writer, took off his hat, stuffed a $20 bill into it, passed it to another writer, and said, "It's for Jackie." By the time Werden's hat passed through the reporters' ranks, it bulged with $2,500—$700 more than the winner's check—for the disqualified champion.

Jackie Pung never captured a major, but among the press and the galleries of women's golf in the 1950s, the Hawaiian golfer won big as the most personable player of her era.

10

Join the Club

The Apple Tree Gang

Gathering in the clubhouse at the end of a round to discuss the day's crisp drives and botched two-footers alike is a golf tradition from St. Andrews in Scotland to St. Andrew's in Yonkers. Fittingly, a man with ties to both sites launched the pastime in America in 1889.

Throughout that year, the rugged-looking gent, whose face was framed by long sideburns and a bristling mustache, gathered with his friends in a six-hole Yonker cow pasture they had dubbed St. Andrew's. At the end of their round, they trooped to a sturdy apple tree where they had hung their coats and a large picnic basket. Dangling from a small chain on one of the limbs was something else—a large silver flask of choice Scotch. John Reid, "the Father of American Golf," pulled down the flask, produced four shot glasses from the basket, and poured a dram in each. Beneath that tree, Reid and his golfing cronies rehashed their round and sipped their Scotch at America's first "nineteenth hole."

Gaiters and Guffaws

Their money already set them apart from most people. And members of America's turn-of-the-century golf clubs wanted to keep most people away from the rarefied air of exclusive courses.

At the same time, the nation's nobs and their spouses wanted something more than a round or a fine meal at their exclusive preserves. From St. Andrew's (Yonkers), to Shinnecock Hills (Long Island), to The Country Club (Brookline, Massachusetts), the affluent vanguard of the Gay Nineties wanted to preen for each other—and for "the help." What better way to show how special they and their club were, the socialite golfers reasoned, than to decree that the men wear special "uniforms" at the club and that women wear the latest in European fashions.

By 1897, Shinnecock had instituted the first waiting list for membership, and one of the things that prospective members clamored for was the honor of wearing the club's distinctive duds. Vanderbilt, Morgan, and other millionaires proudly donned the "distinctive scarlet blazer" with the club's crest. Their wives, daughters, and sweethearts wore jewels and gowns to club functions and the latest outdoor wear—tailored ankle-length skirts, billowy blouses for more freedom of movement when swinging a club, broad-brimmed hats to protect "delicate complexions" from the sun, and gloves to guard against blisters.

At Newport and other competitors for the nation's toniest country clubs, members wore their own "colors," but John Reid and his cronies at St. Andrew's took the top honors for menswear on the course. Into a farmhouse Reid and the others had revamped into a clubhouse they trooped in blue-checked caps, red coats sporting shiny brass buttons, gray knickers, plaid stockings, and gray gaiters. According to a Yonkers, New York, newspaper, commoners who walked by St. Andrew's and spotted the members in their get-ups did stare at the rich golfers' regalia. But the passersby's reaction was not the admiration their better-heeled neighbors craved. Many people laughed at the notion that any man would *choose* to wear an outfit that made him look less like a captain of industry than an overgrown relic of a private school.

Bottoms Up!

They stocked their clubhouses with the choicest wines and liquors and pounded them down with the same relish for which they harangued working-class men. And one of the chief concerns of turn-of-the century country club golfers was to make sure that "the help" never poured the costly beverages down their own throats. Along with greenskeepers, waiters, landscapers, and other hirelings from St. Andrew's, to Newport, to Shinnecock, and to every other golfing preserve of America's moneyed class, the prime suspects when liquor inventories came up short were another form of the help—golf professionals.

Although the rich admired the club professionals' expertise and paid for that knowledge, they never considered them their social peers on or off the course. They were hirelings, pure and simple, there to provide a service. And, many club members charged, golf professionals shared fellow workingmen's thirst for alcohol.

At the 1898 U.S. Open, when club pro Fred Herd won at Myopia, club members were afraid that he would pawn the costly championship trophy for liquor money, and they made him lay down a $200 deposit on the gleaming hardware. They saw no hypocrisy in the fact that many members were staggering occasionally around the clubhouse themselves.

No Peeking

The status of St. Andrew's Golf Club, in Yonkers, New York, as the cradle of the American mixed foursome (see "The Mother of American Golf" in the next chapter) belies the club's erstwhile reputation as a male enclave where, the club historian wrote, "the fair sex [was] tolerated but never welcomed." Further denting the "men-only" image of St. Andrew's early days, the historical record reveals that Rule 11 of the club's original bylaws guaranteed women "the privilege to play on the links on Tuesdays and Thursdays."

According to the bylaws, the women of St. Andrew's also garnered another first, clubhouse access: "The privileges of the clubhouse shall be extended to the ladies, introduced by members, at all times—except on those days which the Governing Committee shall appoint."

In one area of the club, the men tolerated no female presence. The only bar was in the men's locker room. And even when architect Ted Young, who joined the club in 1938, designed a "delightful semicircular bar, with the clock and St. Andrew's emblem over it," the old ways died hard. The club historian noted: "If your wife or girlfriend wanted a drink, obviously they could not gain access to the bar, but were forced to wait in the lobby until someone [a man] appeared who could pass on the order to . . . the bartender."

For decades, a member pointed out, the men worried that "ladies . . . could look into the men's locker room [through double doors swinging open] and see unclad males at the semicircular bar. Fortunately, the height of the bar gave the gentlemen adequate protection!"

One assumes that propriety and not embarrassment fueled the men's modesty.

By 1990s standards, Mrs. John Reid and the other women who struck a ball or sipped lemonade or a cocktail at St. Andrew's at the turn of the century were second-class invites at best, ornaments at worst. No one could argue that St. Andrew's—as well as every other early club except Morris County—was organized as a men's club. Only St. Andrew's, however, can claim America's first mixed four-some and the first bylaw for women golfers. In the club's official history, Desmond Tolhurst points out that "the founding fathers of St. Andrew's did not overlook the women entirely; far from it." He urges "the ladies" not "think harshly of the old St. Andrew's" as a bastion of "militant antifeminists," but as the site where women golfers staked their first claims to America's courses.

Ladies' Day

In the early 1890s, several dozen women in long skirts and an array of plumed, brimmed sun hats assembled on the veranda of the Shinnecock Hills Golf Club. A small, middle-aged Scotsman in cap and tweed jacket then led the ladies from the rambling shingled clubhouse onto the course, but not the twelve-hole course their husbands played. He was either Willie Davis or Willie Dunn, the club professional, and halted the group at the first tee of the layout that he had designed just for the women, the first women's course in America.

Davis, one of Scotland's best golfers and a renowned course architect, had taken a leave of absence from the Montreal Golf Club to lay out Shinnecock's twelve-hole seaside links, lured by the money thrown his way by some of America's wealthiest golf-loving moguls. Dunn came later, in 1893, and expanded the layout to 18 holes. With the Southampton social set's wives and daughters clamoring to get on the links, the tycoons commissioned the design of a second course, for the women. Whether the architect was Davis or Dunn is murky.

One of the Scots integrated a nine-hole design in and around the much longer men's course, marking the ladies' course with red flags that inspired its name, the Red Course. Similarly, he delineated the men's boundaries with white flags, the White Course. The "ladies' course is just about a mile in circuit and does not interfere with the larger course in any respect," *The New York Times* reported.

With bracing breezes from the nearby Atlantic and with sunshine warming them, the women of Shinnecock teed off for the first time on the Red Course.

Although the women were delighted with their own tract, many of them insisted on the chance to play the White Course. The men struck a compromise with them: if a woman could shoot a qualifying score of 95 three times on the ladies' course, she could golf the White Course. In short order, Mrs. Charles Brown, who would win the first U.S. Women's Amateur, in 1895, graduated to the big course, and teenager Beatrix Hoyt's stellar game would soon embarrass most of Shinnecock's men on their own turf.

The One and Only

"There was no other place like this," Sam Cuyler said. "This was the one and only."

"This" was Shady Rest, a Scotch Plains, New Jersey, golf club whose sprawling clubhouse, restaurant, ballroom, locker rooms, tennis courts, and stables seemed to make it the quintessential country club of the 1920s. It was anything but: Shady Rest was America's first such preserve for blacks.

In 1900, the Westfield Country Club took shape as a nine-hole layout just north of a railway line in Scotch Plains. A black neighborhood of small, tidy homes flanked the course, and because local "right of travel" allowed the residents to cross the course to the nearby train station, the club's white membership slowly soured on the club. In 1921, they sold the course to the Progressive Realty Company, run by a cadre of successful black businessmen.

Shortly after the transaction, the new owners announced the

reincorporation of the old Westfield Country Club as Shady Rest, "the first African-American golf club in the United States," and invited all local blacks "to come over" to the course.

Other all-black clubs would sprout up across America in the 1920s and 1930s, but Shady Rest was the only one to offer not only golf and tennis, but also "horseback riding, skeet-shooting, croquet, and social activities that were generally associated with [white] country clubs of the era."

"You could bring your families here, and the kids had a place to play and run around," a member recalled. "Your wife could sit out there on the porch with friends and play cards while we were playing golf. And then after golf, they had a bar. They had a restaurant, and if you wanted to stay overnight, you could dance."

No white clubs of the era offered better musical entertainment than Shady Rest. On weekends, the irresistible chords of Duke Ellington, Count Basie, and Cab Calloway's bands and the magnificent voices of Ella Fitzgerald and other legendary songbirds drifted from the club's ballroom.

Of all the club's attractions, golfers reveled most in the talent of their head professional, John Shippen, the first black to compete against whites and the near-winner of the 1896 U.S. Open. "There was nothing that he couldn't do with a golf ball," a Shady Rest regular noted. Any boy or girl "who wanted to come over and caddie" for Shippen "was free to do so." One, Earl Nettingham, would remember: "Everybody liked Ship, everybody took an interest in him, and he took an interest in the kids. In the beginning we called him Mr. Shippen, but he made it a point to call him Ship. We would follow him around, caddie for him, and when he was working on the greens, we would go out and help him."

In 1932, Shippen greeted a new boss who had just rescued the club from a staggering debt. William Willis, Sr., the owner of a successful taxicab company and a devoted duffer, brought "vision and financial skill [that] allowed Shady Rest to prosper until it became the property of the township of Scotch Plains in the early 1930s."

He would run the club until 1963, overcoming several other financial fiascoes that threatened Shady Rest's survival. "People just kept putting obstacles in his way, saying that the place was closed, that they were going out of business," said his son, Willis Junior. "So to counter that, every week he would have a name band come in out of New York."

Willis Senior was also the man who brought John Shippen to the club and made Shady Rest "a forum for some of the most prominent blacks . . . from all spheres of influence—Althea Gibson, Ella Fitzgerald, W.E.B. Du Bois—and a membership of working-class men and women and their families."

As civil rights cases slowly began to open up public links, Scotch Plains officials worked out a deal with Willis and took control of the club, which was technically a public tract. They changed its name from Shady Rest to the Scotch Hills Country Club, open to all races.

Many of Shady Rest's old members welcomed integration, but longed for "the kind of rapport, relationship, endearment to a black institution" they had found at their own club. They took pride in the course and clubhouse's unique status as the nation's original "black country club," and in the 1986 telecast of the U.S. Open they discovered to their surprise and delight that the man they had known as Ship had nearly seized the Open a century earlier. They had realized that their club professional had been a gifted golfer, but not that the modest man who gave lessons and tended the greens had been a cultural trailblazer.

Today, in the clubhouse at Scotch Hills Country Club, a portrait of Shippen celebrates the legacy of that landmark bond between him and Shady Rest.

11

"You've Come a Long Way"

The Mother of American Golf

Across a Yonkers, New York, pasture on March 30, 1889, history materialized. So, too, did a direct hit to the male ego of "the Father of American Golf," John Reid.

Four golfers, bundled against northeast gusts and blasts of sleet, slogged across the thirty-acre tract with brassies, spoons, cleeks, and putters in hand. Neighbors had grown accustomed to the sight of two of the figures, Reid and John B. Upham, spraying gutta-percha balls around the six-hole course that the duo and other local linksmen had grandiloquently dubbed St. Andrew's.

But passersby on that March day gaped at the other two players, Mrs. John Reid and Miss Carrie Law.

In the 1880s, an era in which entrenched chauvinism held sway, women simply did not venture onto such male turf as a golf course—at least not until Lizzie E. Reid and Carrie Law's landmark round in 1889.

Smacking shots with the hickory-shafted clubs at the sodden greens, the two Yonkers women had joined the boys in America's first mixed foursome. And jumping out to an early lead in the fledgling battle of the sexes was Lizzie Reid, playing against her husband.

Lizzie Reid had seen her husband manifest the first symptoms of golf fever on February 22, 1888. On that day, John Reid and his friend Upham had fired shots at three makeshift holes in Reid's pasture and had launched the game's gospel in the United States, as well as Reid's ascent to the top of the historical leaderboard.

Mrs. Reid was accustomed to her husband's passion for the era's gentlemanly pursuits: shooting, hunting, and tennis. His square-jawed, mustachioed visage was the very image of a sportsman. Reid was a fiftyish, prosperous, self-made iron works executive and had never played golf in his Scottish birthplace, Dunfermline. Finally, in 1888, Scotland's pastime "hooked" him hard.

By April 1888, Reid and his buddies had laid out a six-hole course. Whenever Lizzie Reid needed a word with her husband, she could often find him no farther than the nearby pasture, where, a neighbor recalled, the crunch of clubheads against balls by day forced "any cow who craved a little meadow grass" to do her grazing at night.

Mrs. Reid's evenings sometimes offered no respite from her husband's fondness for that meadow. At a dinner at the couple's home on November 14, 1888, John Reid and his fellow linksters founded the historic St. Andrew's Golf Club.

Whether the wife of the Father of American Golf recoiled at becoming the mother of all golf widows or whether she just wanted to sample the mania in the meadow, Lizzie Reid crashed the men-only course by invitation of her husband.

She and Carrie Law tramped onto the first hole with John Reid and John Upham, assailed by sleet and drizzle that St. Andrew's stodgiest men would have deemed heaven-sent to chase the fairer sex from the course. The two women, made of sterner stuff, took their first swipes at gutta-percha balls.

In the foursome, the Reids did not play as a team: Lizzie Reid was paired with Upham and her husband with Carrie Law. If some minor tiff had separated the Reids for the round, the couple kept the mystery to themselves.

The women, who had never swung a club, somehow escaped a mere golf lesson from the men. Instead, they agreed to a match that John Reid soon would regret.

The foursome's scores mounted amid squalls that weighed down the women's long winter skirts. The cold weather taught Lizzie Reid and Carrie Law what their husbands already knew: a mishit of an iron against a frigid gutta-percha ball sent shock waves surging throughout a player's body.

Such torments notwithstanding, the two women did not beg out of the match as many males of the era might have expected. The pair gamely splashed across the course with their male partners, chasing white Eclipse balls through the muck.

Despite difficulties in lofting the roughly dimpled Eclipses and in reading the course's greens, watery twelve-foot mazes of gullies and bumps, Lizzie Reid's team bested her husband and Miss Law by one hole. The foursome's scoring system required that when a hole was tied, or halved, each side claimed half a point.

In the wake of Lizzie Reid and Upham's soggy one-hole victory, the foursome opted for another six-hole match. As the teams hooked, sliced, and duffed their way across the sopping holes again, the two women once more proved as equal to the elements as the men, the first-round losers striving for vengeance. But when the final putt spattered into the cup, vindication eluded John Reid— by one and a half points.

Reid, ever the sportsman, did not squelch the results of America's first mixed foursome. Later in the day of the match, the minutes of St. Andrew's third official meeting tersely noted: "Mrs. John Reid played with J. B. Upham against Miss Carrie Law and John Reid and beat them by one hole in the first round, and in the second round beat them by 1 1/2 holes."

Although Lizzie Reid and Carrie Law did not realize that they had sounded a clarion call for future golf widows to become golf partners, the two women's legacy would strengthen, as well as occasionally strain, the relationships of generations of links-loving couples.

How did the great John Reid handle his historic defeat? According to attorney Archie Reid, John Reid's great-great-grandson, the Father of American Golf never again played a round against or with his wife, the woman whose *New York Times* obituary in 1922 anointed her "the Mother of American Golf."

Blasted Hopes

In January 1895, Cornelia Howland listened to the news delivered by a tall, silver-haired man who was impeccably attired and groomed. Several minutes later, he departed her Morristown, New Jersey, mansion "a shaken man, pale and mopping his brow," writes Rhonda Glenn. Few socialites had ever seen Paul Revere, great-great-grandson of *the* Paul Revere, so cowed. They knew, however, how formidable Miss Cornelia Howland and her suffragette precepts could be—especially when it came to golf, the matter that Revere had just discussed with her. He had informed her that she had been voted out of her position as president of the Morris County Golf Club.

Howland took the news personally, for she had overseen every inch of the course's construction in 1894. The course had been special—the only all-women golf club in the nation. To Howland, the most crushing news was that the very women with whom she had founded the club had betrayed not only her, but their unique course. Most locals had no doubt that the men had compelled their wives to vote out Howland. One fact was certain: when the vote had taken place, Howland had been absent from the club's boardroom. No one had informed her of the meeting. Neither her friends nor their husbands had wanted to confront her face to face, and once the vote was taken, Revere had been drafted to bring her the news.

In an era when men ruled domestic affairs, Cornelia Howland, a plain, personable, fiftyish dowager, needed no man for financial or emotional support. Educated and refined, she considered no Morristown man her intellectual better. Because she was one of the wealthiest citizens of one of America's most affluent towns, her name appeared on guest lists from New York's brownstones to Newport's mansions. She lived an independent life that some of her socialite friends secretly admired.

By 1894, Howland had tapped golf balls on Newport's putting green, the course's only spot where women were allowed to play. St. Andrew's allowed members' wives limited access to the course, and Shinnecock Hills had built a nine-hole course for women, but as the game's popularity spread across moneyed enclaves in the Gay Nineties, many women of privilege wanted more time on the course than the men allowed them. Women's magazines urged readers to claim increased rounds on courses. "With golf links in every neighborhood," the *Ladies' Home Journal* exhorted, "there is no reason why the middle-aged woman should fasten herself in a rocking chair and consent to be regarded by the youngsters around her as antiquated at forty-five. Instead of that, she can, with her golfing club, follow her ball from link to link, renewing her beauty and youth by exercise in the open air."

The advice was written by a man named John Gilmer Speed, but offered no blueprint for women eager to get on the "links in every neighborhood."

In early 1894, a score or so of women gathered in the Morristown parlor of Mrs. Henry Hopkins, all of them eager to take up golf, but unwilling to be consigned to their local club's putting green. Over tea and pastries, they devised an answer to their dilemma: to hire architects and laborers to build a women-only club. The Morristown ladies elected their group's only single woman, Cornelia Howland, president of the venture, and she went

The founders, in New Jersey in 1893, of America's first all-women golf club, the Morris County Golf Club.

right to work, contracting one of the game's finest course architects, Robert Cox, of Edinburgh, to lay out the Morristown course. Her cronies persuaded their husbands to finance the project, for which Howland signed a healthy check.

In early summer 1894, blue bloods arrived from Boothbay to Charleston for the social event of the summer, a weekend-long celebration of the Morris County Golf Club's grand opening. Among the swells and their wives were several European princes, princesses, and other assorted royalty, and as their Morristown hostesses and hosts took them on a tour of Cox's layout, the husbands of Howland's friends realized that the ladies-only tract was better than any other club in the area. Only the front nine of the 6,030-yard course was completed, but the emerald-hued fairways, stone footbridges, nasty little traps, and manicured greens sculpted across rolling hills and around several creeks convinced Paul Revere and several of his friends that such a piece of real estate was more than the ladies could handle in the long run. For the moment, the Morristown men let the ladies have their day and show off their front nine, graced, in the fashion of the era, with nicknames for each hole. The members' favorites were the Devil's Punch Bowl, the Hoodoo, Setting Sun, and Blasted Hopes, the latter aptly named as events turned out.

As the well-coiffed, well-tailored crowd gathered at the first tee, men sharing glittering flasks and gloved women angling parasols against the sun, Mrs. Arthur C. James teed up a ball and prepared to christen the women-only course. She took a hard cut and missed the ball, nearly falling. Flushing but smiling, she composed herself, addressed the ball, and swiped it onto the fairway. The socialites applauded her "clout," about twenty yards. Eleven strokes later, she was on the green, 238 yards from the tee.

The other players, including Howland, all of them utter beginners, also struggled to connect with the ball. According to the *New York Sun*, Lois Raymond, topping shot after shot, winced and exclaimed: "Isn't that too mean for anything!" Having gathered for cocktails and camaraderie, the gallery cared nothing about the quality of play and bet candy on the earnest but amateurish players, who took the crowds' jibes good-naturedly and kept swinging away.

In the weeks to come until the first snowfall, Howland, Raymond, James, and the rest of the Morristown ladies played their course whenever they wanted, never forced to surrender tee times to men. The women's idyllic rounds, however, were about to change.

In January 1895, about a year after their landmark meeting at Mrs. Hopkins's, the Morristown ladies gathered again to elect a new president. No one had bothered to call Cornelia Howland.

The women voted Paul Revere to the office and demoted Howland to honorary president. They also authorized Revere and his all-male board to incorporate the club and run it as a business.

When Revere delivered the news of the changes to Howland, she refused to accept her honorary post. Only she and Revere knew the details of the conversation that sent him from the house wan and perspiring. Neither she nor Revere revealed what had been said, but one fact was certain: Cornelia Howland, the force behind the Morris County Golf Club, never set foot there again, not even for the 1895 U.S. Women's Amateur Open Championship.

Mrs. Brown's Crown

On November 9, 1895, the finest female player in the United States read thirty soggy feet of the Meadowbrook (New York) Hunt Club green. One long, tortuous putt and a hard-charging rival stood between Mrs. Charles S. Brown and the first women's golf championship in America's annals. She took her putter from her caddie, scanned the green again, and inhaled deeply as she set up over her ball. Then, almost imperceptibly, she drew back the club, nudged the ball toward the cup, and waited.

Just after ten that morning, the thirty-five-year-old Mrs. Brown, wife of a wealthy New York businessman, had strolled from the Meadowbrook clubhouse with twelve other affluent women, all of them avid golfers. They could barely see each other in a dense fog swirling around the course and cloaking views of everything but the first bunker.

As the competitors gathered at the first tee, the tourney's referee, USGA president Theodore Havemeyer, and event organizer Oliver Bird, chairman of the host club, pondered a cancellation. Bird's daughter, May, and the other players persuaded the men to let the women play through. The decision sent applause rippling through the throng of socialites and golfers assembled around the first tee.

The contestants for the prize of a glistening silver cup worth $1,000 readied their drivers, eager to compete for the honor of the five tony clubs represented: Shinnecock Hills; the Essex County Club, in Manchester, Massachusetts; the Morris County Golf

Club, in Morristown, New Jersey; the Newport Country Club; and the home course, Meadowbrook.

As the women squinted down the fairway, unable to spy the flag, and cuffed their first drives of the day into the murk, a *New York Sun* reporter remarked that the competitors had come not only to play, but to show off their fashion sense for "one of the gayest social events that has ever taken place." The newspaperman noted: "The costumes of the ladies were very attractive and pretty. Gray skirts with brown leggings and white, blue, or red waists were the predominating features of the golf costumes."

As pretty as those costumes were, their heavy material, even weightier from the dampening mist, restricted the players' swings to varying degrees. Most of the women also wore woolen waistcoats against the chill, further inhibiting their swing planes. The scores on the first hole reflected the effects of too much fashion on the

Mrs. Charles S. Brown, the winner in 1895 of the first U.S. Women's Amateur Open.

USGA

fairway. Mrs. Brown, possessor of a powerful swing honed on both the women's and men's courses at Shinnecock, staggered through a score of eleven on the first hole. She had plenty of company in her ragged start: four others opened with a ten or worse. Mrs. Fellows Morgan, of the Morris County Golf Club, surged out front with a seven on the par-four, a feat lauded as remarkable because the golfers could only see the flag from fifty yards away. May Bird, who knew the Meadowbrook tract like the proverbial back of her hand, buckled in the fog for a ten. To Mrs. Brown's relief, her most formidable rivals, Miss Nan Sargent, of the Essex County Club, and friend and fellow Shinnecock member Mrs. Arthur Turnure, also carded disastrous scores, ten and nine respectively, on the foggy first hole.

As the crowd followed the players across the front nine, the mist slowly lifted, and from the second to the seventh holes, Brown and Sargent steadied their nerves and their play, pulling away from the pack. Then, on the eighth, a long hole laced with plowed turf whose furrows grabbed golf balls in brutal lies, Brown and Sargent sprayed shots all over the acreage, but they recovered on the ninth. They made the turn onto the back nine with Brown ahead by one stroke over Sargent and by five over Mrs. William Shippen, of the Morris County Club.

Although newspapers reported that the golfers played eighteen without an intermission, women's golf historian Rhonda Glenn believes that the contestants broke for a light lunch after the front nine. When the teacups and fine place settings were cleared, the golfers headed out for the back nine minus Miss Louise Fields. The Morris County player had withdrawn, her arms—as well as her ego—probably sore after flailing at her ball ninety-six times on the first nine holes.

The back nine turned into a duel between Brown and Sargent as Mrs. Shippen fell out of contention. The only player charging within striking distance of the leaders was Mrs. W. B. Thomas, but a twelve on the seventeenth hole finished her hopes.

Brown's game proved a crowd-pleaser, her drives and her approaches steady. Applause twice burst from the crowd for her aggressive play in the second round.

Despite crisp drives and some fine moments with her short game, Brown could not shake Sargent. A play-off loomed going into the final hole.

On the long home hole, Brown needed to get two drives up the long hill. But with the sodden green killing her approach shot's roll, she was left with a seemingly unmakable thirty-foot putt for the victory. A two-putt would leave her tied with Sargent.

Brown studied her shot's possible paths, none of them promising. Then, as the crowd grew quiet, she approached her ball, lined it up, and arranged herself for the first "money putt" of an official women's championship. She pulled her putter back a few inches and pushed her ball on its line—hard. If she lost, she would not lose by leaving her stroke short and wondering, "What if. . . ."

"In a big putt of fully thirty feet," the *Sun's* reporter wrote, Brown "holed her ball nicely, the best putt of the day."

With her clutch shot, Mrs. Charles S. Brown claimed an immortal, unassailable niche in the game's history: her name stands atop golf's leaderboard as the first U.S. Women's Amateur champion. The silver pitcher that she won sits on display today at Golf House Museum, in Far Hills, New Jersey.

That same sportswriter who had witnessed Brown's memorable putt praised "her work yesterday" as "a beautiful exhibition of golfing." He had enjoyed ample chance to scrutinize the "beauty" of Brown's game—all *132* winning strokes' worth. Although her card might evoke laughter from gifted women golfers of the 1990s, one should remember that Brown carried a handicap that would likely have sent the scores of Annika Sorenstam and other present-day LPGA stars soaring: bulky, constricting clothing that, in some cases, included corsets.

No matter that scratch women golfers today can halve Brown's score. All sports have their "magic numbers," and for the future of competitive women's golf, 132 is such a figure—the score that won the first U.S. Women's Amateur Open, Mrs. Brown's crown.

A Star Is Born

A bow affixed to her dark, upswept hair, she stared confidently at the camera's lens. Clad in a dainty lace blouse with a cameo adorning her high collar, seated regally in an ornate chair, clasping a Jack Russell terrier, the teenager presented the very picture of privilege and manners. Eventually, she would settle into the high-society marriage and lifestyle in which she had been raised from Park Avenue townhouses to Newport's seaside mansions. But when the photograph was taken, Beatrix Hoyt was more than just another lovely young socialite: she was America's first homegrown golf star, the winner of the 1896, 1897, and 1898 U.S. Women's Amateurs. As newspapers across the country noted, her game was not quaint rounds in the 130s. Beatrix Hoyt shot in the low nineties—better than most male amateurs and remarkable when stacked against male professionals posting winning scores in the mid-eighties (though it must be pointed out that the men played longer holes).

Hoyt learned the game at Shinnecock Hills, where her parents were members and where club professional Willie Dunn, realizing that the girl had a natural feel for golf, spent hours shaping her long, graceful swing and solid putting stroke.

In 1895, Hoyt took pride in fellow Shinnecock player Mrs. Charles Brown's triumph in the first U.S. Women's Amateur, and the following year, when Brown chose not to compete again, Hoyt was entered to represent her home turf in the 1896 Open, at Morris County Golf Club in New Jersey.

Sixteen years old, she stunned the 1890s golf set with a victory seized with a round of 95 on the longest layout for a women's course.

She defended her silver cup in 1897 at the Essex County Club as a rainstorm turned the seaside Massachusetts course into a morass. Although her final-round score ballooned to a 108, the newspapers, as well as her swing coach, Dunn, called it a remarkable round under almost unplayable conditions.

In 1898, the eighteen-year-old Hoyt, a pretty young woman whose long, dark tresses billowed from their stays whenever the wind kicked up, arrived at the Ardsley Golf Club in New York, to face sixty women intent on wresting her title from her. Her picture having appeared in numerous newspapers, the teen had attained celebrity status. "So far as our home-bred golfers are concerned," praised *The New York Times,* "she is not only in a class by herself, but also superior in the quality of her game to any of our men." Given the prejudices of the era, the writer ignored two American men whose games compared to those of Scottish and English professionals because that pair, John Shippen and Oscar Bunn, were, respectively, an African-American and a Shinnecock Indian. Hoyt herself had seen both men's talent on display at Shinnecock Hills, and, as in her own case, both men's swings bore the trademarks of Willie Dunn, long, powerful swings with a complete follow-through.

The drawing power of Dunn's prize female pupil reached its zenith at the 1898 Open. A thousand of America's high and mighty, as well as a sprinkling of European royalty on tour, streamed from trains and coaches into the Hudson Valley enclave and made their way past towering riverside mansions to the Ardsley Golf Club. "The glittering array of vehicles that unloaded their passengers at the clubhouse door included every type from four-in-hand drags to pony phaetons, and also a horseless carriage with thick pneumatic-tired wheels that conveyed Amzi L. Barber [a well-known tycoon] and his family," the *Sun*'s society scribe reported. The Barbers and other affluent spectators had come not only to cheer on their own clubs' players, but also to see if Beatrix Hoyt's game matched her burgeoning reputation. The *Sun* reporter marveled that even Mrs. John Jacob Astor and her closest friends had shown up to watch the teenage phenom.

As the sixty-one golfers gathered at the first tee beneath a clear blue sky and brilliant sunshine, many among the gallery and social-pages reporters first scrutinized the players' outfits. "The vivid red of golfing coats added life and contrast to the latest autumnal creations of milliners and modistes," the same reporter wrote. Most of the players were more concerned with how they looked in stylish but weighty "fall lines" than with how those garments restricted the golf swing: "The scores were in the inverse ratio to the newness of the gowns."

Beatrix Hoyt would not have won raves for her sportswear that day. She had shown up to play, not to preen, as her "sensible . . . dark brown tailor-made cloth skirt and a pink silk waist, white cravat, and low-cut tan shoes" were about as functional on a fairway as the era's fashions allowed.

From her first drive of the day, Hoyt barely smiled and spoke only to her caddy, Willie Sands, a fine golfer who knew every nook of the Ardsley course. Hoyt opted to defer to his advice without question. "No player ever followed instructions more implicitly," a spectator remembered. "For whenever Sands would mark out the line to be followed, Miss Hoyt would obey him with the most perfect accuracy."

In a line that must have sent suffragettes' collective blood pressure soaring, the same writer lauded: "[Hoyt] buried her own individuality completely, and the two made a splendid team."

To the *Sun,* the most splendid part of Hoyt's game was her ability as an "escape artist":

> A great player is one who can make up quickly for any mistakes, and on the fourteenth hole Miss Hoyt proved her right to be in this category. She nearly made the 235-yard green on the uphill drive and played a mashie [the archaic name for a five-iron] on the second. There was some rough ground before the green.
>
> "You must pitch high, Miss Beatrix: don't try to run!" ordered Sands.
>
> Miss Hoyt followed his advice, getting within fifteen feet of the hole. The putt ran down, the ball going so slowly as it neared the hole that everyone thought it would stop. Both Miss Hoyt and Sands, in the way that golfers have, clucked at it like a horseman to his trotter on the speedway. It was an exciting moment, but the ball had just life enough to reach the hole, into which it toppled like a squirrel darting into a hollow limb.

With "cracking drives" and "sweet run-up shots," Hoyt captured her third straight U.S. Amateur and columns of newsprint from Ardsley to San Francisco. She was as proud of her score, 92, as of her victory, breaking the course record by four strokes. In the 1898 U.S. Men's Open, at Myopia, in Hamilton, Massachusetts, Fred Herd, a renowned British professional, shot two 84s and an 85 in his winning tally, and while no one would say that Hoyt's ability compared to Herd's on the longer, more difficult holes the men played, her shooting in the low 90s was an amazing feat nonetheless.

Hoyt played in two more Women's Amateurs, but stumbled in both. The problem, the *Times* assessed, was not that her game had tailed off, but that other young women of means had closed the gap between themselves and "the heavenly Hoyt." Her last appearance in competition came in the 1900 Women's Amateur, held at her home course, Shinnecock Hills, whose members "had the utmost confidence in their favorite's ability."

Most East Coast newspapers speculated that Hoyt could win again, but that her competition would prove tougher than ever.

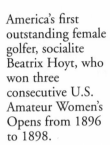

America's first outstanding female golfer, socialite Beatrix Hoyt, who won three consecutive U.S. Amateur Women's Opens from 1896 to 1898.

USGA

Hoyt struggled throughout the opening round, her confidence dwindling as she met Bostonian Margaret Curtis in the semifinals. Peg Curtis, one of a Brahmin millionaire's children, all of whom excelled at golf and tennis, was sixteen, the same age as Hoyt when she had launched her domination of women's golf.

As the twosome hit their opening tee shots, a large gallery of Shinnecock Hills members followed them, believing the hometown support would buoy Hoyt from her erratic play of late. As they headed into the turn, however, Hoyt trailed, a lethargy gripping her game over the front nine.

As the pair followed their drives on the tenth, Hoyt looked at the familiar faces, which implored her to lift her game, and began to deliver. Her friends' and family's support, the *Sun* reported, "brought Miss Hoyt to her senses, and the golf she played on her homeward journey was the finest exhibition of skill that has been seen upon the links this season."

Hoyt charged to a 43 for the back nine, an onslaught that should have buried Curtis's challenge. But "Little Peg" would not buckle, losing a few strokes but holing a putt to salvage a tie on the eighteenth.

A sudden-death play-off loomed, and few spectators believed that Hoyt would lose now to the precocious Bostonian. They tied on the nineteenth, and on the twentieth, Hoyt, straining for a little extra distance, knocked her ball into a bunker. Curtis hit hers down the middle of the fairway. Her face tight, Hoyt squeezed a nice recovery shot back onto the fairway, but could only reach the green in four. Curtis, on in three, two-putted for a five, and Hoyt faced a long putt to stay in the match.

A spectator would recall that utter silence hung above the crowded green as Hoyt took long seconds in measuring her line to the cup. Then she pushed it to the cup. For a moment cheers went up—then they dissolved as her putt stopped over a foot short.

Beatrix Hoyt's reign as the queen of early women's golf in America was over. Twenty years old, she withdrew from competition, although she continued to play a friendly round or two.

The lovely young woman from Shinnecock Hills had been the first golfer, male or female, to spark the press's interest. Other golfers' names and abilities would soon eclipse hers, but none could strip away her status as America's first homegrown links star.

Beyond Our Shores

The Curtis sisters, Margaret and Harriot, thought that they were ready. So did Georgianna Bishop—the 1904 U.S. Women's Amateur champion—Mary Adams, and Frances C. Griscom as they boarded a liner for England to play in the British Ladies Championship, at Cromer. They knew that they were ready to compete as individuals in the tournament, but their real goal was to put American golf on the map in an unprecedented team match—the American women versus the best of the United Kingdom.

In the Open, Britain's Bertha Thompson was the victor, but the match everyone anticipated was the "them against us" competition that followed across the windswept Cromer course. Although the Ladies Golf Union, the ruling body of women's golf in Britain, had pushed for such a competition since 1898, the Americans had demurred, correctly judging that their players were not yet good enough to compete, let alone win.

Just before the 1905 British Ladies Championship, the eight American women posed for a group photo, in which their smiles radiated confidence. That confidence was born of privilege and a passion for sports. Margaret and Harriot Curtis, daughters of a wealthy Boston businessman, had grown up around golf clubs and tennis courts and were now in their early twenties. Margaret, "Little Peg," was considered the up-and-coming star of the Americans. Newspapers praised her game, as "a gift divine," and her charming personality, which masked a formidable competitive will. Harriot was also a gifted player and would win the U.S. Women's Amateur in 1906, one year before Peg dethroned her.

The most flamboyant of the American women was Frances C. Griscom, a Philadelphia socialite with a love of sports and adventure. She shot skeet as well as any man, loved to fish, and was the first fashionable Philadelphia woman to drive and own an automobile. In World War I she would drive a Red Cross ambulance. The winner of the 1904 U.S. Women's Amateur Open, she told her hometown newspapers that if she was on her game, she would beat the British ladies handily.

Griscom, a solidly built golfer who could outdrive many men on the course, as well as behind the wheel of a car, got the chance to back up her boast. Following the British Ladies' Open, she led the American squad, all of them sporting collared white shirts except Griscom, who wore a turtleneck, onto the Cromer course. They paired off in match play against a "who's who" of English, Scottish, and Irish stars, including the great Dorothy Campbell, and May and Florence Hezlet, Britain's own sister act, paired up against the Curtises.

Beneath a steady drizzle and chill gusts, the British ladies drubbed the Americans, six and one. The Curtis sisters reveled in the international team play despite the outcome and sailed home determined to turn the impromptu tournament into a regular event.

Peg Curtis campaigned for organized international competition over the following twenty-five years, battling male officials who contended that her idea would create professional women players, an unseemly idea to golf officials on both sides of the Atlantic. In *The Times* of London, Sir Ernest Holderness, a British Amateur champion, sneered at Curtis's dream: "No one could expect a married woman with young children to win championships. That is a shocking thought. It would be enough ground for a divorce."

Peg Curtis, co-founder of the Curtis Cup, suffragette, and U.S. Women's Amateur champion in 1907, 1911, and 1912.

USGA

Undeterred, Peg Curtis spearheaded an informal America-versus-Britain match the day before the 1913 U.S Women's Amateur, at Wilmington (Delaware) Country Club. She and her teammates put up a spirited fight, losing five and four.

In 1927, the Curtis sisters, backed by female golfers in the United States and Great Britain, purchased an antique Paul Revere bowl and urged the USGA to offer it as the prize for a regular international women's tourney. With a patrician eye for antiques, Curtis was not pleased by the trophy's quality or size, deeming the cup one of Revere's few lackluster efforts; however, it was reportedly the best that could be bought in Boston at the moment. The cup's size, she told a reporter, was not the real issue: "Our chief aim was to do something to accelerate the start of matches with girls overseas."

In 1932, twenty-seven years after the Curtises and their teammates had teed off against their British foes at Cromer, the Curtis sisters' long campaign paid off. Over fifteen thousand spectators mobbed Britain's Wentworth Golf Club to cheer on the British and American women competing in the first official international match that was sanctioned by the USGA and Britain's Ladies Golf Union. This time, the Americans, led by Marion Hollins and Glenna Collett Vare, were ready, avenging the 1905 debacle and carrying home the grand prize—the Revere bowl, the *Curtis Cup*. Peg and Harriet Curtis's vision forged an ongoing tradition for the game.

Both sisters' achievements extended far beyond the golf course. Harriot jumped into the vanguard of the civil rights movement, serving as dean of women at Hampton Institute, a mainly African-American college in Virginia, and later as the secretary of the United Negro College Fund in Boston. Peg worked tirelessly for children's charities and headed the Massachusetts War Production Board's salvaging and recycling campaign during World War II. But no matter how involved she became in charitable and patriotic efforts, Peg Curtis's passion for the links never waned. "Golf is my life . . ." she told *The Boston Globe*. "I'd play it with rocks if I had to."

No Greater Honor

Margaret "Peg" Curtis, winner of three U.S. Women's Amateur titles, a champion tennis player, and later namesake of the Curtis Cup matches, was a crack athlete who grasped that life did not begin and end on a grassy fairway or a grass court. In 1905, the year she first played in the British Ladies' Amateur, she was enrolled in the first class at Simmons College School of Social Work, aiding victims of a fire that gutted Boston's Chelsea district. Most Boston Brahmin women never even considered hands-on contact with the city's poor Irish and Italian immigrants, but Peg Curtis fearlessly walked through their rough, squalid neighborhoods to deliver medicine and food to hard-pressed families.

When World War I broke out in 1914, Curtis did not wait until America's entry into the conflict in 1917 to pitch in with her typical alacrity. She joined the Red Cross in 1915 and was assigned to Paris, where she became chief of the Bureau for Refugees and drove ambulances under fire from giant German cannons known as Big Berthas. Even after the Armistice, Curtis eschewed her golf career and worked for a Quaker relief agency setting up health-care clinics throughout war-ravaged Europe. The sight of the American, with her pinned-back patrician hair and courtly, authoritative demeanor, changing wounded children's dressings and risking her life in the influenza wards of 1918–1919 so impressed the French government that the nation's Assembly awarded her its highest civilian honor, the Légion d'Honneur. In 1958, the recipient said that nothing in her great golf career rivaled that award, which, she concluded, every other wartime relief worker had deserved as much as she had. No other American golfer has earned the Légion d'Honneur, and few have matched her perspective on life.

The "Bewitching Blonde"

The golfer "swaggered along as jauntily as a bullfighter, ready to pounce on any mistake [an] opponent made," a reporter for *The New York Times* lauded. "No handsomer, more gifted athlete ever graced a tournament." This gifted golfer appeared not only atop the game's leaderboard, but also on the cover of *Time,* the first golfer to grace publishing's most vaunted cover. The player's name? It was not Jones, Palmer, Nicklaus, or even Tiger Woods. The name was Edith Cummings.

In 1925, Cummings soared to heights of celebrity that no other American golf great, male or female, had yet reached. She not only became the first golfer to captivate the nonplaying public, but was also the inspiration for one of the most memorable characters in American literature. In *The Great Gatsby,* F. Scott Fitzgerald based his character Jordan Baker—socialite, athlete, friend and confidante of Daisy Buchanan—upon Edith Cummings, "the real-life beauty" who, a *Look* article proclaimed, "far outshines the reigning stage and screen beauties and all other athletes except Babe Ruth."

Fitzgerald depicted Jordan Baker as slim and graceful; she was "a charming sophisticate who gave up cocktails when training for a tournament" and spent hours "reclining on divans and making delicious small talk with the glorious Daisy." He wrote that Baker's grace of movement stemmed from playing on "golf courses on crisp mornings."

Dubbed "a great beauty" and "the Golden Girl of Sports" by *Time,* the "bewitching blonde," a Chicago socialite, was raised in the rarefied world of mansions and private schools, a member of America's elite whose families belonged to the nation's great old private clubs. She had beauty, polish, and natural athletic ability. She also had something else—a passion for golf and a rigorous work ethic when it came to her game. She practiced incessantly, her brilliant smile and flapper airs softening her ferociously competitive nature on the links.

Cummings's talent first materialized for the press in 1921, when, as an eighteen-year-old, she made the cut for the British Women's Amateur. In 1922, she arrived at White Sulpher Springs, site of the Women's Amateur, determined not to just show up, but to win.

The format was match play, head-to-head competition, the pressure growing with each win. Cummings's touch and nerves carried her through the early rounds, her brimmed ribboned hats, her trademark smile, and her tanned blond features captivating spectators. *The New York Times* gushed: "No handsomer girl ever graced an athletic contest. She has Marilyn Miller and Julia Sanderson [silent-screen actresses] beaten a mile for sheer beauty. She looked like a bewitching blonde."

Cummings's first few foes found little about her game bewitching, only intimidating. She trounced her first few foes, roaring to the semifinals, where she would meet nineteen-year-old Glenna Collett.

Collett, trained by Scottish stalwart Alex Smith, possessed the most powerful game among her peers, her backswing fueled by a complete turn like that of the male players. But depending upon the state of her fragile nerves, her game ran from sublime to erratic. At the 1918 Rhode Island Championship, her first tourney, she had finished dead last with a 132. She could knock several drives right down the middle and the next several into the water, woods, and rough. Around and on the greens, her short game was always an adventure.

Going into her round against Cummings, Collett lacked the swagger of the bewitching blonde, but did own a longer and better game—if she could hold her psyche together. Few players would have bet on her chances.

Besides wondering if her swing would hold up, Collett feared

Edith Cummings, the golf champion whose beauty captivated F. Scott Fitzgerald and who became, in 1924, the first golfer ever to appear on the cover of *Time*.

USGA

that her friendship with Cummings would come into play, describing their relationship as one of comrades but great rivals. Both players anticipated a close match in which poise would prove the key, and no one in women's golf possessed more self-assurance than its "golden girl."

On a blustery morning when the winds threatened every shot with potential disaster, Cummings forged a quick lead with steady, safe play, leading three-up as the twosome started the back nine. Many spectators figured that Cummings would dispatch Collett by the thirteenth or fourteenth hole. Cummings, however, began to waver on the greens. After missing several makable putts, she trailed by one as the women headed toward the final green. Both had left their approaches less than ten feet from the cup.

As Cummings and Collett walked across a small stone bridge to the green, both felt the pressure, although Cummings smiled and nodded at the press and the gallery as if the biggest tournament in

American women's golf were not on the line. Continuing to cloak her tension, she strolled up to her ball, a foot farther from the cup than Collett's, calmly read the putt, and buried it. Applause poured from the fans, especially, an onlooker remembered, from the many well-heeled young men rooting for Cummings.

As the ovation ebbed, Collett paced around her ball and marked off the distance to the cup. She still held a one-up lead, but needed to hole the tricky left-to-right putt to win. She tried not to think about what would happen if she missed, as she had done in other tournaments.

According to an interview Collett gave years later to Rhonda Glenn, Collett could not help but look at Cummings, who relished exploiting any foe's miscue. Then, for some reason, Collett glanced at the sun-draped stream flanking the green. "I looked down enviously at the trout sunning among the rocks, happily oblivious of the army of a gallery and two harassed girls laboring under the strain of a ding-dong match."

Collett stepped up to her ball and rolled it into the cup. The moment marked the proverbial turnaround of her career, Collett forever shedding the choke label that had followed her. Cummings smiled and hugged her friend, but, as she admitted later, did so while seething at one that got away. Now golf's golden girl, having thrown away a sizable lead, would have to live with "goat's horns" for a year.

For that next year, Collett was the toast of the ladies' game, winning her second straight Women's North and South Amateur Open, the Palm Beach Championship, the Eastern Amateur, and the Canadian Open Amateur and establishing herself as the favorite for the 1923 U.S. Women's Amateur, at the challenging Westchester-Biltmore Country Club in Rye, New York.

Cummings had played well in several tournaments that year, but had not won. Still the photogenic golfing favorite of the society pages and women's magazines, she played to her glamorous flapper image, but was not up to her best game on the links. Too many late nights, too many bootleg parties, and too many turns on the dance floor, her critics whispered to gossip columnists.

Westchester's more-than-six-thousand-yard layout offered little forgiveness to players off their game even a bit. Beginning with a tricky par-three, the course featured small, tight greens and demanded precise hillside approaches.

To the surprise of no one in attendance, Collett won her first two matches. To the surprise of many, Edith Cummings crushed her first two foes, and a finale pitting the two friends and rivals appeared imminent, a match Cummings craved. She did her part by disposing of her third-round opponents.

In the third-round match-up between Collett and veteran Alexa Stirling, three-time winner of the event, Stirling reached back into her shotmaking past and edged out the younger woman. Although Collett was disappointed that she would not meet Cummings, the deposed champion took the loss with the grace and sportsmanship that would mark her career. She even admitted to the *Times* with admirable honesty that there was a moment "of relaxation and freedom that came with the sudden loss of my title." She hinted that after the burst of celebrity following her 1922 win over the game's golden girl, she had tried to be all things to all people and to outdo or at least match Cummings's popularity.

Despite her own disappointment that Collett had been bounced from play, Cummings could not allow her desire for revenge to affect her game. Alexa Stirling was waiting in the finals.

In what a newspaperman billed as women's golf's glorious past against its glamorous future, Cummings and Stirling navigated the treacherous course with skillful, often spectacular strokes. As the match wound on, however, the younger woman's longer distance began to tell. Finally, when she nudged in her final putt to seize a three-and-two triumph, Edith Cummings flashed her famed smile, a winner's smile this time.

One year later, in August 1924, that champion's smile greeted readers from the cover of *Time*. Not only did golf have its first "glamour girl," but also its first cover girl.

Women's golf would see its share of photogenic players over the years, including such players as the Bauer twins, Laura Baugh, and Jan Stephenson. But only one golfer, woman or man, could claim the sport's first *Time* cover.

In addition to her magazine first, no golfer except Edith Cummings would win a place in classic American literature. Yet she would have been the first to point out one major difference between herself and Fitzgerald's Jordan Baker: the latter cheated during a match. Edith Cummings was as honest as she was bewitching.

12

In Print and Pictures

Here to Stay

In 1895, *The New York Times* noted that "a new outdoor pastime... appears to be gaining favor in this country." The game featured "a white, hard rubber ball 1¼ inches in diameter... and a number of clubs like little boys' rattling shinny sticks." The first members of St. Andrew's, Newport, Shinnecock Hills, and other country clubs might have recoiled at the comparison of their brassies, niblicks, and mashies to a kid's "sticks," but would have welcomed the columnist's ensuing mention of those private preserves as the fledgling centers of American golf.

John Reid and his cronies, who had picked up proper links lingo, surely smiled at the newspaperman's mistaken description of a course's holes, or cups, as "a number of tin basins called goals."

Worth a Thousand Words

James Barnes usually rolled up his sleeves when he went to work. In his usual white shirt and a tie, he looked the very picture of an apothecary or a storekeeper in his native Cornish town of Lelant. But when he bunched up those sleeves, the transplanted Englishman became "Long Jim" Barnes, one of the fiercest competitors and finest swing technicians in early American golf. In 1919, publishing house J. B. Lippincott executives deemed Barnes's swing picture-perfect and signed him up to put that stroke in and on a book's pages. The finished product was not America's first golf book, but it proved the first modern instructional tome, the harbinger of an industry that would fill bookstores' shelves with how-to volumes by golfers from Bobby Jones to Greg Norman.

Among the elite golfers of 1919, tousle-haired, long-faced, long-limbed Jim Barnes was hardly the game's most photogenic player. Though polite, he spoke in clipped phrases whenever possible. A publisher seeking a more charismatic golfer could have chased rising young American star Walter Hagen.

What Jim Barnes lacked in flamboyance or chatter did not diminish what he did offer Lippincott: three bankable assets. Having won the first PGA Open, in 1916 at Siwaney Country Club, in Bronxville, New York, Barnes had appeared in headlines across the nation's sports pages. He also attracted packed galleries as the John Daly of the day, for Barnes had earned his nickname, "Long Jim," not for his rangy build, but for his astonishing length off the tee. His newsworthy name and distance combined with his superb swing mechanics to offer Lippincott a marketable package.

Barnes agreed, but wanted to do a book the same way that he always taught the game—short on words and heavy on example. rs devised a unique approach for Barnes's book, whose succinct title told prospective buyers all they needed to know about the work's contents: *Picture Analysis of Golf Strokes.* The instructional book, just over 250 pages long, offered dozens of photos of Barnes, with tie and bunched-up shirtsleeves, and *showed* golfers every aspect of the swing from setup to finish. Photo sequences also captured Barnes's techniques to head off hooks and slices, as well as his keys to better chipping and putting. Text served as a backdrop, checkpoints for each sequence of pictures. Besides offering readers a detailed photographic study of a sound swing, *Picture Analysis of Golf Strokes* implied that if golfers pored over the photos, they could discover the secret ingredients of Long Jim's distance. The lure proved seductive enough to pry two dollars apiece, a pricey sum for the era's book buyers, from twenty thousand golfers, turning Barnes's little instructional book into one of 1919's best-sellers. It was the first golf-instruction book laden with photos.

As a book critic and golf lover noted, *Picture Analysis of Golf Strokes* was unreviewable in the usual manner because its text made no literary pretense. The photos were the story and delivered everything mentioned in the title. How many readers unlocked the mystery of Barnes's long drives is anyone's guess, but to his peers in 1919 and beyond, the answers were simple: his swing's long, powerful arc and his perfect balance filled each page in black and white.

An Animated Round

In 1948, a new golfer appeared on movie screens across America. His game delighted children and adults alike, as did his sarcastic patter. Unlike other players who clamped their lips around a cigar or a cigarette as they strode the course, this celluloid hero chomped a carrot. He would take up a new game fifty years later, showing Michael Jordan how it's done on the hardwood of *Space Jam.* Bugs

Bunny was the "real thing" on the fairway and on the foul line—or at least the *reel* thing.

Hollywood's most famous rabbit took to the links in the cartoon flick *My Bunny Lies over the Sea,* in which he defeats a kilted Scotsman who would hit a shot and would challenge the rabbit with the tagline "Try and top that." Of course, Bugs does just that.

No right-thinking golfer would attach much significance to a golf cartoon, but this film, aside from the laughs it culled from both kids and their parents, indicated that golf, while still perceived by many Americans as an aristocratic pastime, was gaining a foothold in popular culture.

13

Look Out Below!

Bombs Away!

On May 27, 1928, two golfers gave a whole new meaning to air-mailing their balls down a fairway. Two biplanes swooped a mere fifty feet above a crowd at the Old Westbury Golf Club. As the spectators arched their necks under the cloudless blue sky, the aircraft banked above the Long Island course's first hole, the engines' din deafening. Then a man perched in the rear seat of one of the planes leaned over the fuselage and tossed something toward the green. Seconds later a golf ball crashed several feet from the cup.

From the second plane another ball plummeted, landing a few yards off the green. Both planes headed for the second hole, and again two balls dropped toward the green. Before the aircraft roared away from the course, they had "strafed" the front nine. The "bombers," M. M. Merrill and Arthur Caperton, both members of Old Westbury, had completed their mission: to drop balls as close as possible to each cup. Below, Merrill's partner, William Hammond, and Caperton's, William Winston, moved toward the two balls on the first green, putters in hand. The game's "ground troops," Hammond and Winston had the job of mopping up aerial golf's pitch-and-putt zone.

Merrill had proved a fine bombardier, hitting every green. Caperton, however, had dropped three balls into deep rough, leaving Winston with several tough lies. Precision bombing won the match, three-up, for the Merrill-Hammond pairing, who had converted easy putts as Winston thrashed about in the rough.

Newspaper accounts of aerial golf spurred other clubs to give it a try, and in July 1928, the Dunwoodie Golf Club, in Yonkers, landed a name player for its first airborne assault on the course. Congressman Fiorello La Guardia, however, opted to serve as the grounded golfer, leaving teammate and pilot J. P. Maloney to fire away from above. The politician and pilot defeated three other teams—"flying circuses," according to an unimpressed and sarcastic *New York Times* sportswriter—one-up. Although La Guardia's name would become that of one of the world's most famous airports, his connection to air golf was fleeting.

The game itself proved equally ephemeral, golfers preferring to launch their own tee shots rather than airmail them, even if the latter method eliminated slices and hooks. Golf in the clouds went the way of goldfish swallowing, flagpole sitting, and other curious pastimes of the Roaring Twenties.

The Flying Wedge

"Wee" Bobby Cruickshank could taste it—a U.S. Open triumph after a decade of falling just short. The worst of it had been his last-hole play-off loss to Bobby Jones in the 1923 Open. Now, as the jockey-sized Scot struck his drive on the eleventh hole of the Merion Golf Club, in Merion, Pennsylvania, he led the third-round action by two strokes, having played near-flawless golf and showing no signs of tailing off on the final eight holes of the 1934 Open's third round.

The rest of the field knew that Cruickshank would not lose his nerve, for he had endured and overcome too many setbacks to view the links as a life-and-death arena. On the Western Front, he had watched helplessly as a German artillery shell tore apart his brother. Shortly afterward, Cruickshank was captured and deposited in a prison camp where typhus was killing droves of Allied soldiers daily. He cut his way through the wire, stole across several hundred miles of enemy territory, and crawled through the minefields of no-man's-land to reach British lines again. Offered a chance to return home to Scotland, he opted to rejoin his unit in the trenches. The "yips" and jittery nerves bedeviled others at Merion that day but not the diminutive survivor of the Western Front.

Cruickshank was calm as he watched his drive come down on the eleventh, but he had never craved a win so much in a career that included numerous victories, although never a U.S. or British Open crown. His tee shot looked good, straight and laying up safely in front of a stream that flowed in front of the green. His ball hit the fairway and stopped dead, perfectly positioned except for one thing: the ball was stuck in a divot.

Still, when Cruickshank studied his lie, he was not worried. His ball was embedded in the turf, but playable if he could dig deeply enough with his club.

Cruickshank attacked at a severe angle meant to carve the earth and explode the ball from the divot, but his clubhead dug too far down, and the ball squirted high and short. It hovered above the creek for a seemingly endless moment and then dove into the water. The tiny splash signaled Cruickshank's vanishing lead. Or so he thought.

The ball hit a rock just below the surface, caromed onto the green, and rolled within a few feet of the cup. Cruickshank gaped for a moment. Then a smile creased his deeply lined face as the gallery's cheers erupted all around him.

He sensed that finally his major was at hand. With a shout of "Thank you, Lord," he tossed his club as high as he could heave it and waved to the crowd. An instant later the club crashed head down against Cruickshank's skull and knocked him cold.

Slowly, he came to, his white linen cap torn by the club and lying nearby. A huge welt was rising on his head, and, as his eyesight was blurred and he had trouble recalling where he was, a doctor tending the wound told him that he had to go to a hospital. That was fine, the Scot muttered, but not until he had won the Open. He refused to withdraw.

Cruickshank wobbled through the final eight holes, his two-stroke lead vanishing as his scorecard swelled to a 77 for the round. He lurched back to the clubhouse, persuaded the doctors to let him play the final round, and shot a 76 to finish in third place, behind winner Olin Dutra and runner-up Gene Sarazen.

Cruickshank never won a U.S. Open, but at Merion he proved to everyone what his fellow professional golfers already knew: no

While leading the 1934 U.S. Open, Bobby Cruickshank recorded a majors first. Celebrating a lucky shot, he tossed his club into the air, hit himself on the head, and knocked himself out. He lost.

USGA

golfer, not even raucous Walter Hagen, rivaled Wee Bobby Cruickshank for toughness, or for the proper perspective about rising above adversity. Although the Scot was disappointed by the bizarre conclusion of the 1934 Open, he related to a reporter that the loss "wasn't much" compared to his wartime ordeals.

In the aftermath of Cruickshank's accident, the USGA levied a ban against blatant club-flinging in any of the organization's tourneys. The rule still applies, perhaps Bobby Cruickshank's painful legacy to the game.

From Fairway to Airway

A famous player climbs into a private plane, flashes a million-dollar smile at the pilot, and settles back into a plush seat to be jetted off to the Tour's next stop. As much an executive as a golfer, the Tour great is as likely to scan *The Wall Street Journal* as to stretch out for a nap as the plane streaks off. The journey was not always so easy, so comfortable, as now, when Greg Norman, Tiger Woods, and other modern golf greats relax in their own Gulfstreams and other private jets. And chances are that if today's Tour greats were asked who first took the game aloft, the answer, Johnny Bulla, would cause a few to scratch their heads or stare quizzically.

In December 1945, Ben Hogan and several other golfers stepped aboard a large transport plane. A broad-shouldered, square-jawed man was perched in the cockpit, his left hand on the throttle, his headphones in place. He greeted the golfers with a grin that oozed assurance, the same grin he had flashed when accepting his check as winner of the 1941 Los Angeles Open. In 1939 and 1946, he had fallen just short to finish second in the British Open.

Like most Tour professionals, Bulla had formerly loaded his clubs and valises into a car and had driven thousands of miles a year to get from tournament to tournament. With the risk of disqualification if players arrived at an event an hour or two late, twenty-four hours nonstop behind the wheel was commonplace for some professionals. A flat tire, an empty gas tank, or any conceivable mechanical glitch could cost even the best players in the best autos a chance at the prize money that helped keep that car and that golfer on the road. Bulla, like most professionals, had often pulled his car into a club exhausted and so close to tee time that he could not get a few hours' sleep or a practice session and would shoot a ragged first round. In late 1945, he came up with a solution: he bought his own plane.

Bulla did more than just purchase the cargo plane. He flew it. During World War II, he had piloted transport planes, discovering that his touch with a throttle rivaled his skill with a golf club. He would remark that heading from the fairway to the runway seemed only natural.

Flying his plane was the easy part for Bulla. The cost of keeping it aloft was something else, as in most tournaments of the day a player had to finish no worse than tenth to win even a meager prize. In a hands-on example of the American entrepreneurial spirit, Bulla offered to fly fellow players to tournaments if they shared the costs of fuel and upkeep.

Bulla's proposal intrigued his peers, but some balked at first, wondering if Bulla, who was one of the Tour's best-liked players but considered one of its flakes, was a man to entrust with one's life. Some players wondered if the pilot, who played a dime-store ball rather than the top-of-the-line balls of the era, had been similarly frugal in the purchase of his plane.

The gregarious Bulla convinced a handful of players that his horseplay in the clubhouse and on the practice tee meant nothing in the cockpit. When several players boarded "Air Bulla" and arrived safe and on-time for tournaments, word spread on the Tour

USGA

PGA Tour player Johnny Bulla flew his fellow golfers from tourney to tourney in his own plane in the 1940s.

that Bulla was an even better bet as a pilot than as a putter. Even white-knuckled Tour passengers would literally put their lives in Bulla's hands. Fanatical about maintenance, checking every inch of his plane before takeoff and immediately after landing, Bulla may not have been the best player on the Tour but was its best pilot.

While other players read newspapers and magazines in the club-house, Bulla pored over flight charts and weather reports. He never took other players aloft if a storm loomed, and told them to drive to the next event. Amazingly, in his decade of flying fellow profes-sionals, not one player could ever relate a frightening flight when Bulla was at the controls. "Air Bulla," however, was a Spartan oper-ation, with players crammed in uncomfortable seats and bundled up against the cabin's chill. Even though Bulla kept his plane on course, the twin-engined transport bucked at turbulence more noticeably than the larger passenger planes. He urged professionals with weak stomachs or any airborne "yips" to stay on the ground. But, with his unbridled self-confidence, he often took off alone in bad weather—and always arrived in one piece.

Some of today's high-flying pros make more appearance money for one event than Johnny Bulla made in his entire career. But it was Bulla, not Norman or Woods, who first took the game from the fairway to the runway.

14

A Hothead and a Hula Dancer

The Profane Pro

His nickname sounded so benign, but the words that burst from "Wiffy" Cox's lips shocked staid galleries of the 1930s. When he hooked or sliced a drive or pushed a putt away, his face would redden and language more common on the docks of Cox's native New York than on the fairways and greens of America's most exclusive country clubs erupted.

Cox had grown up in an Irish-Italian Brooklyn neighborhood, learning to talk tough and to back it up with his fists when necessary. Like other immigrants' sons in New York, future on-course rivals such as Gene Sarazen (Saraceni) and Tony Manero, Cox rode the trains to Westchester County to lug the golf bags of players on private courses, and, like many other caddies, sneaked in rounds with clubs borrowed from the pro shop and developed an outstanding game. Other caddies who competed for players' tips with Cox and nickels and dimes in their after-hours rounds before heading back to the city discovered to their discomfiture that Cox's short stature was eclipsed by a shorter fuse.

Luckily for Cox, as a 1930s reporter wrote, the golfer's fine game spoke even louder than his big mouth. He finished in the money in many tournaments in the late 1930s, but his break-through came with his victory over a strong field in the 1931 North and South Open, a tournament ranking just a notch below the U.S. Open in importance.

In 1934, Cox stomped, swore, and shot his way to a tense tri-umph over Ben Hogan and Byron Nelson in the Texas Open, the crowd teeming with rough-around-the-edges millionaire oilmen who cheered on the foul-mouthed golfer as a kindred soul.

Before the 1935 Agua Caliente Open, in Tijuana, Mexico, Cox posed for a photograph with a mariachi band near the desert club-house, and in his tie, sweater, windbreaker, and crisply pleated slacks the smiling golfer appeared the antithesis of his hot-tempered repu-tation. If onlookers had not known that the pleasant-looking man with the receding hairline was Wiffy Cox, they might never have noticed him in the crowded photo.

Once Cox teed off, any doubts about his volcanic temper evap-orated in a rush of mutterings and curses that ebbed and flowed with the success of his round. His demeanor was better than usual at the Mexican tournament, for he played some of the best golf of his career to grab the game's richest prize—the Agua Caliente's $15,000 winner's share.

The man with the foulest mouth on the fairways eventually took the head professional job at one of the nation's most beautiful and traditional clubs, Congressional, in Bethesda, Maryland. He soon learned to tone down the profanity when giving lessons to members: he wanted to keep the high-paying job.

On October 21, 1939, Cox arrived at Congressional early in the morning, as usual, and encountered a sight that would cause his temper to blaze, and that would enrage the club's membership every bit as much as Cox. Skunks had torn up the course overnight.

Cox, with a white-hot single-mindedness, grabbed a rifle, prowled the course that night, and shot thirty-three skunks. He received the club's thanks and piles of letters from outraged animal lovers.

No Hula Allowed

On August 30, 1952, laughter and cheers pealed from the gallery at Waverly Country Club, in Portland, Oregon. USGA officials were not amused. Jackie Pung, who had just won the U.S. Women's Amateur over Shirley McFedden, was not only celebrating the win with a wide smile, but also saluting her homeland, Hawaii. Officials had said nothing when Pung draped a lei around McFedden at the trophy presentation, but now the Honolulu golfer had broken into a victory hula and was gliding languidly across the green.

As her dance continued, tournament director Totten P. Heffelfinger, clad in a dark business suit, arms folded, had seen enough. He walked up to Pung and whispered something. She nodded and, to the disappointment of the crowd, a wire service reporter wrote, "stopped shimmying."

Heffelfinger had momentarily reined in the irrepressible Pung, but her smile and good-natured demeanor made her a gallery favorite for years to come. Her solid but flamboyant game would entertain the LPGA galleries of the 1950s and would spark a far greater controversy five years later (see "Read 'Em and Weep").

15

"Show Me the Money"

Connecting the Dots

Long before the Nike swoosh and Greg Norman's shark materialized on golf courses worldwide, the Dot ruled links logos. It made
its debut in 1906, the advertising gimmick of the A. G. Spalding &
Bros. golf division, emblazoned on a simple white background—
the ball itself.

From the moment that a barrage of print ads and billboards proclaimed the arrival of "Spalding Red, White, and Blue Golf Balls,"
stores struggled to keep them in stock even at an astronomical $6 a
dozen in an era when $25 take-home constituted a good salary. Part
of the ball's allure was Spalding's performance guarantee:

> These are the best golf balls made in every aspect.
> The longest and truest flyers.
> Accurate in approach work.
> Deadly in putting.
> The toughest and most durable of covers.

The source of the ball's success lay in that durable cover, where
a small red, white, or blue dot was painted. The "Red Dot" and the

"Blue Dot," which was also known as the Spalding Wizard, were popular, but the Spalding White proved the most popular, not because of its plain-hued dot, but because of its sound when struck by a club. As a golfer connected with the White Dot, the ball gave off a sharp click, proverbial music to a golfer's ears and to those of Spalding executives.

A 1906 advertisement for Spalding's high-performance "Dot" golf balls.

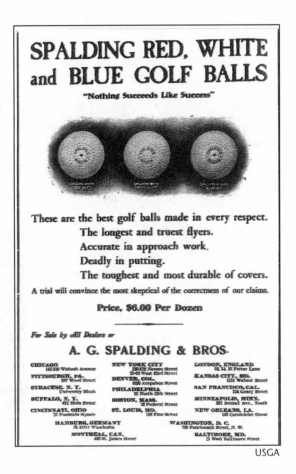

SPALDING RED, WHITE and BLUE GOLF BALLS

"Nothing Succeeds Like Success"

These are the best golf balls made in every respect.
The longest and truest flyers.
Accurate in approach work.
Deadly in putting.
The toughest and most durable of covers.
A trial will convince the most skeptical of the correctness of our claims.

Price, $6.00 Per Dozen

For Sale by All Dealers or

A. G. SPALDING & BROS.

USGA

"Nothing Succeeds Like Success," trumpeted Spalding's publicity for the Dot Balls, and, especially in the case of the "Click Ball," the admen's claim proved true. The company had proved that for golf equipment sales, the packaging was as important as the product, a lesson not lost on future sporting goods giants.

Whitewash

In 1907, the golfer approached the ball, focused on just the right spot, and took a stroke—with a small paintbrush. He prepared the ball for another round by applying custom-made golf-ball paint, for a second, third, or any number of new coats to cover the areas chipped or flaking from its last round. For hardware stores, the union of paint and "pellets" was lucrative.

When golfers bought new balls, they shone as whitely as they would in the 1990s, but not for long. Several shots into a round, a new ball looked as though someone had scuffed it around for years. By the eighteenth hole, a good golfer's ball was pocked, and a hacker's ball was missing most of its coat. The remaining white surface quickly yellowed.

As always, entrepreneurs turned out a stream of "solutions" that ranged from chemical glazes to dyes to seal the ball with so-called special properties. Most golfers, however, preferred the paints sold in hardware stores, "whitewashes" such as Castle Brand Golf Ball Paint, which promised that its product "does not turn yellow or chip off the ball." The whitewash's makers neglected to inform buyers that its "guarantee" expired long before the life of the ball.

USGA

A 1907 ad for ball paint, without which, in the game's early days, no golfer's equipment was complete.

Improved technology would solve the paint problem by the 1930s, but until then, players who considered painting golf balls too plebeian found their own solution: let a caddy do it.

Cardboard Cash

Let someone else do the work, and then cash in by adding one's own angle to the original product. Countless fortunes have tapped into that theme. In 1910, an entrepreneur scrutinized another man's golf brainstorm and patented a new twist to the original. A. W. Hill took Dr. George Grant's design for a golf tee and wrapped it in a cardboard collar inscribed with Hill's name.

As his patent application explained, Hill's "tee sleeve" was not a tee itself, merely an attachment on which a message could appear. The message that he envisioned was anything an advertiser wanted to emboss—for a fee.

Cheap to produce and costing buyers mere pennies, Hill's tee sleeves caught on with businesses and individuals alike, everything from company logos to "sweet nothings" captured on cardboard. Until 1922, Hill turned cardboard into cash. Then, with the invention of the wooden tee, advertisers could emblazon their messages on the tee itself, rendering Hill's notion as disposable as his material.

Although A. W. Hill's name has disappeared from the game's annals, his vision of the tee as a billboard, business card, personal effect, and even a memento (for a price, of course) of such legendary acreage as St. Andrews Old Course flourishes.

Dough for the Doughboys

Eighty years ago, a Scottish pro in a jaunty cap and sweater stood atop the American golf world. Or did he? Jock Hutchison's stellar performance at Whitemarsh Valley Country Club's long-distance links, near Philadelphia, on June 21, 1917, netted him neither the customary check for the U.S. Open nor the official title of Open champion. For his victory had come in the 1917 Patriotic Open, and debate continues on whether the national tournament of that war-torn year was a bona fide U.S. Open or an ersatz version. One fact about that Open, however, is indisputable: it helped begin the tradition of golf for a good cause.

In late April 1917, Harry L. Ayer read a disheartening letter from USGA secretary Howard F. Whitney. Ayer, chairman of Brae Burn (Newton, Massachusetts), that year's Open site, learned that the USGA had decided to cancel the Open because of the war. However, Howard W. Perrin, USGA president, announced on May 22, 1917, that a "National Open Event [was] to be held at the Quaker City as a patriotic event from June 20–22." Perrin, in denying Brae Burn the so-called National Open and scheduling the tournament at Whitemarsh, had moved the event to his own hometown, Philadelphia, and his own club, opening himself to charges of cronyism.

If any New Englanders wanted to cry foul, Perrin's blueprint for the Patriotic Open took the proverbial wind from their sails. Perrin required that professionals play not for payment, but out of pride and patriotism. The Red Cross would receive all the prize money, and tournament officials would charge admission fees projected to raise up to $5,000 for the army's field-hospital service. Brae Burn officials could hardly complain without appearing unpatriotic.

In the wake of the USGA's announcement that the tournament would be a charity event, cynical reporters doubted that many golfers would play for free: "Among the professionals," *The New York Times* asserted, "interest in the substitute tournament seemed to be at a low ebb."

The press utterly miscalculated golf's stalwarts. On the eve of the tournament, the *Times* acknowledged its "surprise to see such a notable array of professional talent, nearly 100 golfers," at Whitemarsh. One, Jock Hutchison, a native of St. Andrews,

Scotland, but a naturalized American citizen, had lobbied hard on behalf of the Patriotic Open.

Absent from the field was 1916 Open and Amateur champion Chick Evans, but he was doing his bit on June 17 in a patriotic best-ball foursome at the Flossmoor Club, in Chicago. Up-and-coming Walter Hagen had entered the Whitemarsh field late, but was on his way.

As Hutchison, Alex Cunningham, Tom McNamara, "Long Jim" Barnes, the rest of the professionals, and such amateurs as Norman Maxwell walked to the first tee in front of a large gallery on June 20, gusts swept the course. By round's end, wind-tossed shots had caused several favorites' scores to soar into the 80s. Only seventeen professionals and one amateur carded scores in the 70s, Cunningham topping the leaderboard with an amazing 74, Hutchison in a three-way tie for second at 76. The wind had blown crowd favorite Barnes's prodigious drives all over the tract in a round of 84 that had infuriated Long Jim.

Two hours after Barnes finished, he informed the tournament committee that the official scorer had mistakenly tagged him with an extra shot on the fifth hole. His partner, George Low, concurred. Barnes threatened to walk out unless the stroke was shaved; the committee refused his demand. Barnes chose to stay in the tourney.

Many of Barnes's fellow pros contended that since the officials had taken a hard line against Long Jim, they should take a similar stance on late arrival Hagen, who intended to catch up with two rounds on June 21. The committee barred his entry.

In the second round, Jock Hutchison carded a 73 as winds again raked the 6,283-yard course. Edward Loos's flurry of crafty clubwork pushed him into second with a 73, one stroke behind Hutchison. Three strokes behind lurked Cunningham.

On the Patriotic Open's final day, two rounds, Hutchison blew away the field with a memorable performance. "Steadiness and

Jock Hutchison, the
Scottish-born winner of
the 1917 Patriotic Open,
the wartime replacement
for the U.S. Open.

USGA

brilliancy . . . his watchwords . . . this son of Scotland went about his
task," a *Times* reporter marveled. Tom McNamara launched a run,
but fell seven strokes short because "[Hutchison's] shots, whether
long or short," were "so sure."

"Never," wrote the reporter, "did almost perfect golf appear
more easy" than in Hutchison's play. To the cheers of a huge gallery,
Hutchison had ensured that the Patriotic Open had matched the
"quality of entry to that for which it is substituted."

Hutchison had conquered the field, but many would contend
that he had not won an official U.S. Open, but merely a lively substitute. What no one can argue is that he and the rest of the
Patriotic Open field had done themselves and the USGA proud.
They had pitched onto the greens of Whitemarsh and had pitched
in for the doughboys.

In the 1990s, the legacy of the Patriotic Open shines in charity
and fund-raising tournaments across America.

Sand Dollars

Gale-force gusts whipped sand into golfers' eyes and blew their balls off tees. Thousands of spectators wearing scarves or turning up collars against the sand squinted to follow shots' arcs through dust clouds. As some of the world's finest golfers trudged down fairways pocked with rocks and scrub and toward greens flanked by deep sand traps, the players could only dream of the well-manicured courses that usually hosted professional tournaments. None of the players, however, wondered why they had made the trip to Tijuana, Mexico: the 1930 Agua Caliente Open offered the richest prize in the history of golf. For $25,000 in the midst of the Depression, Gene Sarazen, Horton Smith, Walter Hagen, "Young Turks" Craig Wood and Paul Runyan, and Chicagoan Jim Foulis, a son of the *1896* U.S. Open winner, were willing to tramp across a course described as an arid wasteland.

To the twenty-seven-year-old Sarazen, the choice to pull out of a winter circuit tourney and head across the border had been especially simple. Already the winner of a U.S. Open and two PGA Championships, Sarazen had racked up substantial earnings, but had lost most of his money in the Great Crash of 1929. He was willing to play a bad course for a crack at the unheard-of $10,000 first prize.

On January 20, 1930, Sarazen and over fifty of the era's best golfers gaped at just how rugged the Agua Caliente tract was. The course was long, 6,735 yards, a par-71, but the distance did not necessarily favor the big hitter, because between tees and greens, rocks, shrubs, and gullies scarred the fairways. Several holes wound through canyons. Typical of the course was the 550-yard eighth hole, whose boulder-strewn, cracked terrain looked more like a lunar landscape than a golf hole. Still, the players figured that their shotmaking skills could conquer the course as long as the desert winds did not rise.

As the golfers trooped in threesomes to the first tee on January 20, 1930, they relaxed a bit, because the sky was clear and because the rain-soaked tract should play soft, preferable to worries about drives and long irons taking bad bounces off sunbaked, rock-strewn desert fairways and into rough that gave a whole new meaning to the word.

The players guessed wrong. Few scored easily, shots biting deeply into rain-softened sand and putts dying yards short of the cup on soggy greens. Only one competitor, Ed Dudley, scraped together a par 71. Tour legend Walter Hagen, his putting touch trapped in the worst slump of his career, struggled to a 78. Sarazen came up short on several approaches en route to a 78. Given the course's obstacles, seven strokes to make up was a long shot.

When the field began the second round, on January 21, they found a different set of obstacles. Dry crosswinds and a warm sun had baked the course, and the gusts picked up speed. Drives and approaches that had splashed to a quick stop the previous day ricocheted off the fairways and past the greens. No one shot par, several players limping off the course with 72s. One of them, Los Angeles professional Olin Dutra, held a one-stroke lead, but fourteen others were bunched within four strokes of the top.

The next day, a gale ripped caps from players' and spectators' heads and sent scores soaring on every hole. Not even the longest drivers could reach the par-four greens in two, and on the first hole, 435 yards, every player got an unappetizing taste of what lay ahead: only four parred the hole; the rest shot bogeys.

All that day, shots caromed off rocks, plummeted into gullies, skittered into sand, and skidded all over the greens. Horton Smith's ordeal on the eighth hole symbolized every player's frustration. He nailed his drive through the crosswind, and when it stopped in the center of the fairway, he faced an easy approach to the green. He marched up to the ball, measured his shot, and swung; his club smacked into a large, half-buried stone. Shock waves rippled up the shaft and his arms, and the ball popped straight up and rolled just forty yards. Smith ended up with a triple-bogey seven on the hole.

With the rocks and the gale tormenting the golfers, no player shot lower than 76. The man who netted that score, Al Espinosa, had needed several lucky bounces to shoot his five over par. Gene Sarazen had skied to a 79, but, going into the final round, trailed Espinosa and Smith by only three.

On the morning of the last round, the sun again washed across Agua Caliente, but the winds had dwindled to a mere breeze. Having navigated the scarred, sandy course for three rounds, the players knew where to air it out and where to lay up, and, without the wind in their faces one moment and at their backs the next, seven golfers were bunched up down the stretch. The unprecedented winner's take fueled the race.

From the first hole on, Gene Sarazen attacked the course, his drives and irons long and firm. But his long putting truly put the pressure on the other six hanging on in the hunt for $10,000.

With all seven players separated by only two strokes as Sarazen coaxed in a fifteen-foot birdie putt on the fifteenth, the money, the Associated Press reported, "was on the table, there for the taking."

Sarazen wanted to take it. On the sixteenth, his ball lay thirty feet from the cup. The safe play was to leave his first putt a little short on the fast green and tap in for a par. He went right for the cup with a long, twisting putt that dropped in the hole for a birdie.

On the seventeenth, he ignored the safe play again and snaked in another birdie putt, heading to the eighteenth two strokes ahead of Espinosa and Smith.

Sarazen hit the green in two, and, now, with a long putt staring at him, he knew that unless Espinosa or Smith eagled the par-four hole, a par for Sarazen would net the $10,000. He calmly holed it and walked off the course, one of the worst he had ever played, with the game's biggest purse.

In front of the clubhouse, tournament officials presented the grinning Sarazen his winnings—$10,000 piled into a wheelbarrow.

Although Espinosa and Smith had fallen two strokes short of Sarazen's birdie blitz, the runners-up also had reason to smile. The $3,750 that each player had earned was nearly double the winner's take in most tournaments.

For the next eight years, the Mexican tournament remained golf's richest. The players loathed the sand, rocks, and winds of Agua Caliente, but loved the wheelbarrow piled with cash. Golf's first big-money open slowly forced America's clubs to increase prize money or risk losing the best players to other courses with bigger coffers.

The Ralph W. Miller Golf Library

Gene Sarazen collects his winnings at the richest tournament to date, the 1930 Agua Caliente Open in Tijuana, Mexico.

A Born Saleswoman

She did not possess the beauty that companies had traditionally sought to sell their products. She did, however, have an engaging smile, a playful sense of humor, and a way of drawing anyone into conversation. Helen Hicks was the type of personality that 1930s Hollywood always cast in the role of the starlet's best friend. But on the golf course, she commanded marquee value: in the 1931 U.S. Women's Amateur, twenty-year-old Hicks had dethroned the era's greatest American female golfer, Glenna Collett Vare, ending the champion's three-year stranglehold on the title. A year later, as one of Vare's teammates in the first Curtis Cup, Hicks played a pivotal part in defeating the United Kingdom squad at Wentworth Golf Club, in England. The British galleries of over fifteen thousand winced as their team lost, five and a half to three and a half, but were captivated as much by Hicks's playful banter with them as by her long drives and touch around the green.

Someone else noticed Helen Hicks's smile and personality. L. B. Icely was a bottom-line businessman who believed that the right personality meshed to the right product meant profits. The hard-nosed head of Wilson-Western Sporting Goods, he had inked Gene Sarazen in 1933 to tout the company's golf equipment in exhibitions, clinics, and tournaments. With Wilson's women's golf lines lagging in sales, Icely had been pondering promotional offers to several notable female players, but did not want to hire a society sort whose appeal might be limited to country club golfers. Although the Depression was ravaging commerce, more middle-class women were taking up the game, in part because equipment, lessons, and even many clubs' memberships had decreased in price. Icely targeted Helen Hicks, of middle-class roots and world-class personality, as the perfect pitchwoman for Wilson's most afford-able, as well as most expensive, equipment for female golfers.

Helen Hicks, U.S. Women's Amateur Champion of 1931, became the first female golfer to sign an endorsement contract, with Wilson Sporting Goods in 1934.

USGA

Icely had chosen shrewdly. Hicks, unlike several other stars of women's amateur golf, not only wanted to compete on the course, but to make a living at it. Bessie Fenn, Helen MacDonald, May Dunn, and a handful of other great players had given up their amateur status, their right to play in USGA events, to cash checks as professional instructors or to work in pro shops. For these working wives and mothers of the 1930s, only three events remained open: the Titleholders, the Western Open, and the Women's Texas Open. The nation's most prestigious women's tournament, the U.S. Amateur, banned professionals and would not budge from the stance.

Having won that event and having claimed her niche in amateur golf, Hicks signed with Icely and became the first woman to reap an endorsement deal, as well as the first U.S. Women's Amateur champion to turn professional. For Wilson, she traveled the country to give clinics at private and public courses with the company's equipment and attire. Although Wilson promoted the clinics and exhibitions as "ladies' days," which drew hundreds of women and girls to the events, many men showed up to see how Hicks's game compared to that of the "stronger sex." She coaxed and challenged the biggest guys in a crowd to a long-drive contest. With her large frame and fluid swing, she outdrove most of the boys, and, with her ever-present grin, told the applauding women that her Wilson driver gave her distance and could do the same for them.

Hicks then took spectators and prospective customers through a swing lesson in which she used every Wilson club in her bag to launch shots of every loft, from every lie, and of every angle. Wearing her trademark beret and baggy sweaters, she punctuated clinics with self-deprecating humor that not only played well to socialites and middle-class women alike, but also sent them off to buy Wilson equipment.

Whenever Hicks's road show landed in Minnesota, an aspiring young golfer attended, scrutinizing Hicks's swing and her persona. "I used to watch Helen Hicks because she had a marvelous personality and did an outstanding job," recalled Hall of Famer Patty Berg. "Anytime Sarazen or Helen Hicks was around my area, I'd be there watching."

Icely and Wilson counted on just those sentiments from the golfing public, and Hicks never disappointed. The bottom line? Helen Hicks sold not only countless clubs, but the game itself.

16

It's Never Too Late

The Wright Stuff?

In 1869, an elderly Scot stopped short in front of a Boston sporting goods store. Several golf clubs and gutta-percha balls sat behind the glass of the show window, and the man walked into the store and asked the proprietor, George Wright, where the closest golf course was.

Wright replied that there was none around Boston. The Scotsman bought the clubs and balls anyway and marched off to City Hall to obtain a permit to mark off a course in a public park. According to Wright, the customer was soon whacking the balls around one of the city's parks.

Nearly six decades after Wright's sale to the Scot, newspapers around the country picked up a United Press article sent over the wires from Palm Beach, Florida, and proclaiming Wright, an "old Boston ballplayer," as the "Real Father of American Golf." At the annual banquet of the Old Guard Society of Palm Beach Golfers on February 23, 1926, Wright, an avid player, revealed that "when he was running a sporting goods store in Boston after retiring from baseball in 1869, he heard of golf and imported a few clubs and balls." As his audience listened raptly, the seventy-nine-year-old speaker, silver-haired and still possessed of the wiry frame of his years as a sure-fisted shortstop for the old Boston Red Stockings, claimed that golf had spread from his long-ago sale to its present "golden age" on the American sports scene and that he, not John Reid or anyone else, was "the man responsible for the general intro-duction of the Scotch game into this country."

Wright convinced his Florida links cronies, but no one else. One sale in a sporting goods store did not sell the general golfing public on Wright's contention, his chief claim to fame remaining on the diamond rather than the course.

An Ageless Wonder

As a wavy-haired, wiry man stepped up to Augusta's first tee, the gallery erupted in cheers. It had been over twenty years since the Scottish-American golfer had headed into a final round atop the leaderboard, a spot he had once claimed regularly. Now, on December 2, 1937, the man whose command of every stroke had cowed opponents in the pre–World I era had one more chance to make golf history. Fifty-four-year-old Jock Hutchison could win the PGA's first Senior Open Championship—if he could stem the charge of an old foe and nemesis, former U.S. Open champ Fred McLeod.

Bobby Jones, who had designed the course with architect Dr. Alistair Mackenzie and, in 1934, had begun the Masters Tournament tour, had lobbied the PGA to bring back the game's old-timers in a nostalgic Seniors Championship. With the aid of wealthy, golf-mad Southern businessman Alfred S. Bourne, who put up a $1,500 silver trophy and a cash purse, the PGA announced that the first annual Senior Open Championship would take place from November 30 to December 2, 1937.

As word got out that Jones and Bourne were offering past greats one more chance to hear a gallery roar and compete for money on each putt, entries came in from all over America. Fred McLeod, Alex Campbell, and other golf greats grabbed their clubs and headed to Augusta for one more chance to stand atop a professional leaderboard.

In Chicago, one of the early century's greatest course craftsmen took up Jones's offer to compete against old foes. Jock Hutchison, a naturalized American citizen who had learned the game on his native St. Andrews' Old Course, had won three of his day's majors—the 1920 PGA Tournament and Western Open and the 1921 British Open, at his old haunt, St. Andrews. He had narrowly missed winning two U.S. Opens, but had captured the controversial 1917 Patriotic Open, the wartime version of the U.S. Open.

Hutchison did not arrive in Augusta to shake the hands of former foes, exchange "war stories," or entertain galleries with wistful flashes of his swing's old magic. The transplanted Scotsman came for one reason only—to win. And he firmly believed that he still had the game to tame Jones and Mackenzie's open fairways and lightning-fast greens.

On the morning of December 1, 1937, Hutchison stepped up to the first tee. Applause greeted him from the packed gallery, but Hutchison, natty in his crew-neck sweater, cuffed trousers, and two-toned spikes, ignored the cheers, no hint of a smile on his sunburned, deeply lined face.

"Old Jock," taciturn as always, had on his "game face." But did he still have his game? Fans who had seen Hutchison in his heyday waited for his drive. He answered with his familiar quick swing that cracked the ball dead center.

Hutchison had served notice. He was not there to entertain nostalgic fans or to rekindle the old days for himself. He was there to win.

Hutchinson was not alone in his confidence that he could still compete with anyone on any course—even Augusta. Tom Boyd,

Charlie Hall, and hometown "boy" David Oglivie matched Hutchison stroke for stroke most of the day. And when the Scot's putting touch deserted him for a spell of three-putts on the back nine, his card soared to 76, four over par and a stroke behind Boyd, Hall, and Oglivie. Tied with Hutchison was Fred McLeod, one of the smallest players in the game's annals, but one of its finest ballstrikers.

Fuming, having perhaps misread Augusta's greens, Hutchison realized that the greens would not be his only natural challenge in the second round. The wind was up, swirling about the course, placing additional pressure on older players who could not hit shots through the gusts as they had twenty years ago. Club selection and touch would prove even more important that second day.

For the first twelve holes, Hutchison played nearly flawless golf. Once noted for his uncanny knack of hitting approach shots with the perfect amount of backspin, he negated the tricky greens by nestling shot after shot within a few feet of the cup.

At round's end, Hutchison held first place, four strokes ahead of McLeod. The Scot, however, had faded on the back nine, carding a 75, three over par.

On Thursday, Jock Hutchison emerged from the clubhouse in his once-familiar position—atop the leaderboard as a championship's final round began. But he wanted more than to hold on to his lead—he wanted to prove to younger pros that he could shoot par on Jones's course. On the final day of the first Masters, in 1934, Horton Smith had won with a final round of par, and now, four years later, Hutchison had a chance to win Augusta's second inaugural tournament.

With each hole of Hutchison's round, the groundswell of gallery cheers grew. That he was pulling away from the field seemed less important than the way in which he charged toward a milestone victory. Though his drives and long irons lacked the yardage of his prime, he coaxed his approaches close to every pin, his shots so sure and soft that many young professionals might have exchanged their longer-hitting games for the fifty-four-year-old's wizardry around and on the greens. Young fans who had never seen Hutchison in his day stared at vintage Jock.

Hutchison shot his par and captured the first PGA Senior Championship. As he accepted the $500 check and clutched the shimmering silver championship cup, forty inches high and soon to be emblazoned with the name of America's first Senior champ, Jock Hutchison, the winner, finally smiled.

Hutchison had done far more than step into the winner's limelight for one last time. He and his fellow over-fifty crowd had proved not only that they could still play scratch golf, but that they could also draw a crowd—a *paying* crowd. In the 1990s, as the Senior Tour's popularity and prize money continue to swell, Nicklaus, Palmer, Irwin, and company owe thanks to Jock Hutchison, Fred McLeod, Alex Campbell, and the rest of the field at Augusta in 1937.

Sources

In researching *Links Lore,* I relied upon many sources. The following were among the most useful.

Newspapers ranging from the 1700s to the present day provided much material for the book. Especially helpful were *The New York Times;* the *New York Sun;* the *New York Herald; The Augusta* (Georgia) *Chronicle; The Boston Globe;* the *Chicago Daily Herald;* the Chicago *Sun-Times;* the *Indianapolis Star; The Miami Herald;* the *Los Angeles Times;* the *Newport* (Rhode Island) *Daily News; The Philadelphia Inquirer;* the *San Diego Tribune;* and the *San Francisco Chronicle.* Also useful were dozens of other newspapers large and small from every corner of America. For many of the stories, old copies of *The Times* of London, the Edinburgh *Evening News,* and *The Scotsman* (Edinburgh) were a gold mine.

Turn-of-the-century golf magazines, America's first, offered colorful and enlightening material of the days when the game first gained a solid foothold in our nation. Several early-1900s publications—*Golfers Magazine, The American Golfer, Golfing, Golf and Lawn Tennis,* and *Golf,* which was not the ancestor of today's *Golf Magazine*—vividly chronicled the sport itself, notable players, and developments good, bad, or strange in club-and-ball technology. By 1905, Spalding printed its tenth annual *Golf Guide;* each issue offered a window on period golf.

Advertisements touting clubs, balls, swing aids, and myriad other golf gadgets then and now provided a wealth of material. So, too, did the spate of early golf biographies, autobiographies, instructional tomes, and even golf-humor books.

Harper's Weekly, Ladies Day, Time, Look, Life, Photoplay, and many more popular magazines were terrific sources of personality and trend pieces about the game.

The U.S. Patent Office provided copies of golf patents that covered everything from the first tee to a radioactive ball.

Golf House, the library and museum of the United States Golf Association and home to *Golf Journal's* invaluable archives, is an unparalleled resource for anyone researching the game's past, present, and future.

At the Boston Public Library, the New York Public Library, and other libraries from Yonkers, New York, to repositories in London and Edinburgh, I found a wealth of material.

From Grantland Rice to Herbert Warren Wind, David Barrett, Al Barkow, and Peter Dobereiner, golf has been blessed with writers of immense literary talent. Mr. Wind's *The Story of American Golf* (1975), *Thirty Years of Championship Golf* (1990), and many other books and columns were cornerstones of my research. The same is true of David Barrett's *Golf Almanac* (1994) and his pieces in *Golf Magazine.* Al Barkow's *Golf's Golden Grind: The History of the Tour* (1982) and *History of the PGA Tour* (1988) illuminate the origins and growth of the professional game. In *The Glorious World of Golf* (1973) and *Preferred Lies about Golf* (1989), the inimitable Peter Dobereiner offers any student of the game's past a feast of facts and anecdotes.

In my "A Place in the Sun" section of *Links Lore,* quotes in the stories about the struggles, heartaches, and triumphs of African-American golfers come from Al Barkow's *Golf Illustrated* pieces and his groundbreaking book *Gettin' to the Dance Floor: An Oral History of American Golf* (1986). Trailblazing golfer Charlie Sifford's enlightening *Just Let Me Play* was also a chief source for my book.

For the history of women in American golf, Rhonda Glenn's magisterial *The Illustrated History of Women's Golf* (1991) is the bible.

For names, dates, and places, the following works proved essential: *The Encyclopedia of Golf* (1964), by Nevin H. Gibson; *America's Golf Book* (the editors of Golf Magazine, 1970); the *USGA Record Book, 1895–1959* (1981); and the *USGA Record Book, 1960–1980* (1981).

Parts of pages 43–48, 72, and 191–195 first ran in *Golf Journal,* parts of pages 1–4 and 146–149 in *Golf Magazine.*

Index

A-Bomb, 107
ABC Radio, 62
Adams, Benjamin, 32–36
Adams, Mary, 162
Adirondack Mountains, 51
African Americans (golfers), 41–52, 59–68, 72–87
Agua Caliente Open, 186–187, 195, 197–198
All-American Open, 59, 61, 75
Aluminum-plated clubs, 91–92, 92*
American Lefthanders Golf Association, 131
Anderson, Dale, 84
Anderson, Willie, 132
Anti-False-Move Machine,108–109
Anti-Semitism, 58
Aoki, Isao, 56, 57
Apawamis Club (Rye, N.Y.), 95, 121
Ardsley Golf Club (Ardsley-on-Hudson, N.Y.), 158–160
Armistice (World War One), 166
Army Air Force, 14

Article Three (PGA Charter), 59–61, 64–65, 67–68
Asami, Rakuze, 56–57
Aspen Grove Cemetery (Burlington, Iowa), 112–113
Associated Press, 15, 52, 54–55, 117, 197
Astor, Mrs. John Jacob, 159
Atomic Era, 108
Atomic golf, 107
Augusta National Golf Club, 5, 14, 86, 117, 203–206
Ayer, Harry L., 192

Baker, Jordan, 167, 172
Baltusrol Golf Club (Springfield, N.J.), 11, 27–29, 70
Barber, Mr. and Mrs. Amzi L., 159
Barnes, James "Long Jim," 50, 174–175, 193
Barnum, P.T., 75
Barron, Carla, 58
Barron, Herman, 58–59
Basie, Count, 144

*Photo citations appear in italics.

Bauer twins (Alice and Marlene), 172

Baugh, Laura, 172

Beil, William, 106

The Belfry Hole (Shinnecock Hills), 46

Bell, Marion, 111

Bell, Thomas Andy "Dude," 111–113

Bell, William, 110–111

Bens, Samuel, 103–104

Berg, Patty, 201

Besselink, Al, 84

Bible, 31, 36, 75

"Big Bertha" (driver), 131, 166

Bing Crosby Pro-Am, 135

Bird, May, 153, 155

Bird, Oliver, 153

Bishop, Georgiana, 162

Blasted Hopes Hole (Morris County Golf Club, N.J.), 152

Blinkers, 100, 101

Blue Dot Ball, 188

Blue, Ira, 62

Boomer, William, 102

Boston, 26–27, 88–89, 161–163, 165–166, 202

The Boston Globe, 165

Boston Red Stockings, 203

Bourne, Alfred S., 203–204

Boyd, Tom, 204–205

Brackenridge Park (San Antonio), 52

Brady, Father Joseph, 36

Brae Burn Country Club (Newton, Mass.), 192

Brassie (club), 1, 91–92, 111, 115

Braverman, Harry, 66

Bridgeport Gun Company (Conn.), 91

British Ladies Amateur, 161–162, 166, 168

British Ladies Golf Union, 165

British Amateur (Men's), 95–96, 121, 164

British Open, 79, 121, 126–127, 179, 181

Bronx Bombers (N.Y. Yankees), 130

Brown, Mrs. Charles S., 143, 153–157, *154*

Brown, Dewey, 48–52, 67

Brown, James Ross, 99–100

Browning, Robert, 25

Bruntsfield (Edinburgh, Scotland), 11

Buchanan, Daisy, 167

Buckwood Inn (Penn.), 50–51

Bugs Bunny, 175–176

Bulla, Johnny, 134, 181–184, *183*

Bunn, Oscar, 43–46, 158

Bureau for Refugees, 166

Burlington Golf Club (Iowa), 112

Burlington Hawkeye, 112-113

Burlington News, 2

Burnett, Mary, 26

Burnett, William, 26–27

Calhoun, Charles H. Jr., 124–125

Calloway, Cab, 144

Cambridge University (England), 26

Campbell, Alex, 204, 206

Campbell, Dorothy, 164

Campbell, Willie, 126–128

Canada, 27, 66

Canadian Amateur Open, 170

Canadian Open, 13

Canterbury Golf Club (Cleveland), 134

Caperton, Arthur, 177–178

Captains Courageous, 2

Carney, George C., 101–102

Carnoustie (Scotland), 117

Carnoustie Swing, 116-117

Carroll Park (Baltimore), 41–42

Casper, Billy, 82–84

Castle Brand Golf Ball Paint, 190

Cedar Crest Country Club (Dallas), 54

Cedar River Golf Club (N.Y.), 51

Century Country Club (White

Plains, N.Y.), 38–39
Chase, Mrs., 152
Chicago Tribune, 74
Chicago Women's Golf Association, 74–76
Church of England, 26
Civil Rights Movement, 67, 86, 145, 165
Clark, Euell, 65
Cleary, Joseph Officer, 37
Cleek (club), 11
Click Ball, 189
Clifton Golf Club (Baltimore), 41
Clinton, President Bill, 26
The Cloister Hole (Morris County Golf Club, N.J.), 46
Collett (Vare), Glenna, 168–171
Columbia University, 103
Community Chest, 73
Congressional Country Club (Bethesda, Md.), 79–80, 186
Conroy, Frank, 37–38
Cooper, Harry "Lighthorse," 11
Cornwall (England), 174
Costner, Kevin, 15, 23, 130
The Country Club (Brookline, Mass.), 126, 139
Cox, Robert, 151
Cox, Wiffy, 185–187
The Crater Hole (Shinnecock Hills), 46
Credit Island Country Club (Davenport, Iowa), 20–21
Cromer (England), 162–165
Cruickshank, Bobby, 178–181, *180*
Cudone, Carolyn, 72, 77–78
Cummings, Edith, 169–172, *169*
Cunningham, Alex, 193
Cunningham, Thomas, 15
Curtis Cup, 164–166, 199
Curtis, Harriot, 162–165
Curtis, Margaret (Peg), 162–166, *164*
Cuyler, Sam, 143

Cypress Point (Pebble Beach, Cal.), 135

Daley, Arthur, 20
Daly, John, 107, 174
Daly, Joseph F., 34–35
Daly, Joseph H., 20
Demaret, Jimmy, 65–66
Davenport Country Club, 16–17
Davis, William, 98–99
Davis, Willie, 44, 142
Day, Reverend C.O., 2
Delagi, Judge, 38
Del Monte Course (Monterey, Cal.), 54
Del Paso Country Club (Sacramento), 78
Dent, Jim, 67–87
Depression, 38–40, 135, 195, 199
Detroit Free Press, 74
The Devil's Punch Bowl Hole (Morris County Golf Club, N.J.), 152
Dey, Joe, 18, 76–79
Diegel, Leo, 122–124, *123*
Dot Ball, 188–189, *189*
Doyle, Sir Arthur Conan, 2
Driving Iron, 91
DuBois, W.E.B., 145
Duck Creek Golf Course (Davenport, Iowa), 16–17, 20
Dudley, Ed, 196
Dunfermline (Scotland), 147
Dunn, May, 158, 200
Dunn, Willie, 44, 46, 119, 126, 128, 142, 157
Dunwoodie Golf Club (Yonkers, N.Y.), 178
Dutch (early golfers), 24–26
Dutra, Olin, 180, 196

East Lake Golf Course (Georgia), 116–117
Eastern Amateur (Women's), 170

Eclipse Balls, 114, 148
Edinburgh (Scotland), 111, 151
Edinburgh University, 111
Eisenhower, Mrs. Mamie, 22
Eisenhower, President Dwight
    David, 22
Elder, Lee, 48, 51, 67-68, 87
Electric Eye, 104–106, *105*
Ellington, Duke, 144
Emergency Work Bureau, 38
Englewood Country Club (N.J.),
    132–134
Espinosa, Abe, 52–55
Espinosa, Al, 52–55, *53,* 197–198
Essex County Golf Club (Mass.),
    132, 133, 153, 155, 158
Evans, Chick, 193

"Fairway Bandit" (dog), 38
Farley, Floyd, 106
Father of American Golf (*see* Reid,
    John)
Featherie Ball, 27
Fenn, Bessie, 200
Fenway Golf Club (Scarsdale,
    N.Y.), 58
Fields, Louise Mrs., 155
Fiero, Teunis, 5, 39–40
Fitzgerald, Ella, 144–145
Fitzgerald, F. Scott, 167–168, 172
Fitzjohn, Ed, 4, 6
Fitzjohn, Val, 4, 6
Five Farms Country Club
    (Baltimore), 124
Fleck, Craig Wood, 16
Fleck, Jack, 15–23, *22*
Fleck, Lynn, 16–18, 20, 22–23
Flossmoore Club (Chicago), 193
Forest Hills Ricker Course
    (Augusta, Georgia), 117
Forest Park Golf Club (Baltimore),
    41
Foulis, James, 46,47
Foulis, Jim, 195

Four-Sided Putter (*see* Davis,
    William), 98–99, *98*
Franklin Park Golf Course (Boston),
    88
Furgol, Ed, 68–72, *71*

Gay Nineties, 5, 44, 139, 150
Gehrig, Lou, 130
Geiger counter, 107–108
General Electric, 104–105
Gibson, Althea, 145
Gibson, Leland, 134
Gleason Park (Gary, Ind.), 81
Glenn, Rhonda, 77, 149, 155, 170
Golf Ball Paint, 190, *190*
Golf Course Superintendents
    Association of America, 51
Golf House Museum (Far Hills,
    N.J.), 19, 156
Golf Journal, 51
Golfers Magazine, 94
Golfologist, 118
Goodrich, B.F., 107–108
Grant, Dr. George F., 88–91, 191
The Great Gatsby, 167
Greater Greensboro Open (North
    Carolina), 86
Gregory, Ann, 61, 72–81
Gregory, Percy, 73, 75
Griscom, Frances, 162–164
Guldahl, Ralph, 52
Gulf Stream (jet plane), 181
Gunter, Madison, 62–63
Gutta-Percha Ball, 1–3, 28, 111,
    114, 146, 148, 202
Gutta-Percha Tee, 90

Hagen, Walter, 9, 10–11, 48, 50,
    54, 56, 90, 123–124, 130, 174,
    181, 193, 195–196
Hagerty, Justice, 39, 40
Hall, Charlie, 205
Hammond, William, 177–178
Hampton Institute (Virginia), 165

Harbor Hills Golf Club (N.Y.), 29–31
Harding, President Warren G., 50
Harmon, Claude, 134
Harrison, Dutch, 134
Harvard Dental School, 88
Haskell Balls, 94
Havemeyer, Reverend John, 33–36
Havemeyer, Theodore, 43–45, 153
Hawkins, Robert H., 50
Heffelfinger, Totten P., 187
Hebert, Jay, 84
Herd, Fred, 140, 160
Hermitage Golf Club (Richmond, Virginia), 14
Herreshoff, Fred, 121
Het Kolven (*see* Kolf)
Hezlet, Florence, 164
Hezlet, May, 164
Hicks, Helen, 199–201, *200*
Highlands (Scotland), 25, 98
Hill, A.W., 191
Hillcrest Country Club (California), 66
Hilton, Harold "Chip," 120-122, *121*
Hindi (language), 1
Hockmeyer, Captain Otto, 30
Hogan, Ben, 10, 16–21, 23, 48, 58, 61, 65–66, 69, 186
Holbrook, Harry, 114
Holderness, Sir Ernest, 164
Hollins, Marion, 165
Holmes, Sherlock, 2
Honolulu, 56, 187
The Hoodoo Hole (Morris County Golf Club, N.J.), 152
Hopkins, Mrs. Henry, 150, 152
Hot Springs (Virginia), 5
Howland, Cornelia, 149–153
Hoyt, Beatrix, 143, 157–162, *161*
Hunter, Dave, 132–134
Hutchinson, Jock, 191–194, *194*, 203–206

Icely, L.B., 199–201
Indians (Shinnecock), 29, 44–45
Ingram, Calvin, 74
Iron Ditto (club), 26–27
Irwin, Hale, 206

James, Mrs. Arthur, 152
James, Mrs. Darwin, 31–32
Jameson, Betty, 132, 137
Japanese Golfers (first to play in U.S.), 56–57, 90
Japanese Open, 56
Jenks, George, 109
Jewish (first to win a PGA event; *see* Barron, Herman)
Joe Louis Invitational (*see also* Louis, Joe), 74
Johnson, Clara Shippen, 45
Johnson, Howie, 84
John Shippen Foundation Scholarship, 48
Jones, Bobby, 9, 13, 57, 116, *116*, 167, 174, 178, 203–205
Jordan, Mrs. Curtis, 79, 80
Jordan, Michael, 175
J.P. Lippincott (publisher), 174
The Jungle Books, 2
Just So Stories, 2

Kellogg, Judge Charles, 34–35
Kentucky, 14
Kipling, Carrie, 1, 2
Kipling, Rudyard, 1–4
Knight, Arthur Franklin, 93–95, 97–98
Kolf, 24, 26

Labatts Tournament, 66
La Guardia, Congressman Fiorello, 178
Ladies Home Journal, 158
Ladies Golf Union, 163
Laffoon, Ky., 134
Lake Merced Course (California), 56

Law, Carrie, 146, 148
Law, John E., 41–42
Lazzeri, Tony, 130
Legion d'Honneur (award), 166
Lelant (England), 174
Little Green and *Little Red Books*, 117
Little, Lawson, 134
Littler, Gene, 18, 70–71, 82
Lofter (club), 91
Londino, Lawrence, 48
The London Times, 164
Long Island (New York), 43, 444, 139, 177
The Longacre Hole (Shinnecock Hills), 46
Long Beach Open (California), 82, 85–86
Look Magazine, 167
Loopers (caddies), 27–32, 38–41, 113–115, *114*, 190
Loos, Edward, 193
Los Angeles Open, 61, 79, 82, 87, 181
Louis, Joe, 59–65, 83
Low, George, 49, 193
Lowell, Dr. William (*see also* tee), 90–91
Lower Course (Baltusrol Golf Club), 71
LPGA, 36, 156, 187
Luminous Ball, 102–103

MacArthur, Reverend Stewart, 35–36
Macdonald, Charles Blair, 44–46
MacDonald, Helen, 200
MacKenzie, Alister, 203–204
Madison Golf Club (N.J.), 49
Maiden, Stewart, 116–117
Maloney, J.P., 178
Mamaroneck (*see* Winged Foot)
Manero, Tony, 11–13, *12*, 185
Mary, Queen of Scots, 26

Mashie (club), 1, 91, 115, 173
Massachusetts War Production Board, 165
The Masters, 9, 14, 17, 59, 61, 65, 68, 79, 86, 203, 205
Mather, Cotton, 26
Maxwell, Norman, 193
May, George, 14, 61, 75–76
Mayer, Dick, 70
McCoy, Eddie, 27–29
McFadden, Shirley, 187
McLeod, Fred, 204–205
McNamara, Tom, 193–194
Meadowbrook Hunt Club (N.Y.), 153–155
Melhorn, William "Wild Bill," 9–*10*, 56
Meridian Hills Country Club (Indianapolis), 72, 76
Merion Golf Club (Philadelphia), 178–179
Merrill, M.M., 177–178
Merrins, Johnny, 62
The Mews Hole (Shinnecock Hills), 43, 45, 120
Midiron (club), 91
Mid Ocean Club (Bermuda), 130
Miller, Marilyn, 168
Mills' aluminum clubs, 91
Miniature golf, 25
Miyamoto, Tomekichi, 56–57
Mohawks, 27
Monti, Eric, 82–84
Moore, Ann (*see* Gregory, Ann)
Moore, Henry, 73
Moore, Myra, 73
Morgan, Mrs. Fellows, 154
Morgan, John Pierpont, 119–120, 139
Morris County Golf Club (Morristown, N.J.), 48–49,142, 149, 151, *151*, 153–155, 158
Mosk, Stanley, 66, 67
"Mother of American Golf" (*see*

Reid, Mrs. Lizzie), 141, 146, 149
Mount Pleasant Golf Club (Baltimore), 41
"Murderer's Row," 150
Musselburgh (Scotland), 126–128
"My Bunny Lies Over the Sea" (cartoon), 176
Myopia Hunt Club (Hamilton, Mass.), 140, 160

Native American golfer (*see* Bunn, Oscar)
National Match Play Championship, 56
National Negro Championships, 82
Naulakha (Vermont—*see* Kipling, Rudyard), 1–4
NCAA Championship, 15
Neckbone Circuit, 50, 67, 81, 85
Negro Baseball League, 50
Nelson, Byron, 58, 186
Nettingham, Earl, 144
New York Sun, 152, 154, 156, 159, 160–161
The New York Times, 5, 16, 19, 28–30, 34–35, 38, 40, 44, 53, 56–57, 59, 62, 70–71, 74, 78, 102–103, 120, 127–128, 133, 137, 143, 149, 158, 160, 167–168, 170, 173, 178, 192, 194
New York World, 24, 26
New York World's Fair, 106
Newport Country Club (Rhode Island), 128, 139–140, 150, 154, 157, 173
Niblick (club), 91, 111, 115, 173
Nicklaus, Jack, 62, 167, 206
Nike, 188
Norman, Greg, 107, 174, 181, 184, 188
North Shore Country Club (Illinois), 55
North-South Open, 186

Oakland Open, 62–63
Ocean County Hunt and Country Club (Lakewood, N.J.), 4–6
Ogilvie, David, 205
Ohio, 108
Old Guard Society of Palm Beach Golfers, 202
Old Westbury Golf Club (N.Y.), 177
O'Leary, Paul, 62
Oliver, Ed "Porky," 134–135
Olympic Club (San Francisco), 15, 17, 20
Ozaki, Jumbo, 57

The Plateau Hole (Shinnecock Hills), 46
Palm Beach Championship, 170
Palmer, Arnold, 13, 15, 23, 167, 206
Palmer, Johny, 13–15
Park, Willie, Jr., 126–128, *127*
Park, Willie, Sr., 126
Patriotic Open, 192–194, 204
Peete, Calvin, 67, 87
Penick, Harvey, 117
Perrin, Howard W., 192
Perth (Scotland), 25
PGA, 10–11, 13–17, 36, 48–69, 74, 82, 86–87, 115, 122–124, 126, 135, 174, 183, 195, 203–204
PGA Senior Championship, 206
Phoenix Country Club, 58
Picture Analysis of Golf Strokes (*see* Barnes, Jim), 175
Plainfield Country Club (N.J.), 90
The Plateau Hole (Shinnecock Hills), 46
Pocatello Country Club (Middleton, N.Y.), 39
Portage Country Club (Akron, Ohio), 108
Progressive Realty Company, 143
Pung, Barnette, 136–137

Pung, Jackie, 136–137, *136*, 187
Putnam, Kingham H., 114

Quick, Smiley, 62

Radar Gun, 106
Radioactive Ball, 108
Rake-Iron (*see* Brown, James Ross), 99–100, *100*
Ramsay, C.T., 101
Rawlins, Horace, 44, 46
Rawls, Betsy, 136–137
Raymond, Lois, 152
Read, Robert, 94, 97
Red Course (Shinnecock Hills), 143
Red Cross, 163, 166, 192
Red Dot Ball, 188
Red Scare, 108
Reddy Tees, 90
Reid, Archibald, 149
Reid, John, 33, 103, 110, 113–114, *114*, 126–127, 138–139, 146, 148–149, 173, 203
Reid, Mrs. Lizzie, 141, 146–149
Revere, Paul, 149–153
Revere Paul Bowl, 165
Reynolds, Jim (*see* Electric Eye), 104–105, *105*
Rhode Island Championship, 168
Rhodes, Ted, 61–65, 67, 81–82, 84–85, 87
Richmond Golf Club (California), 62–63
Roaring Twenties, 50, 55, 130, 178
Robichaux, Jolyn, 77, 81
Robinson, Jackie, 47, 81, 83, 86
Rockefeller, John D., 48–50
Rowell, John, 63–64
Royal and Ancient Golf Club of St. Andrews, 96, 98
Royal Montreal Golf Club, 142
Runyan, Paul, 195
Ruth, Babe, 129–131, *129*, 167

Ryall, Ernest, 117–118
Ryder Cup, 54, 59

Saegkill Golf Course (N.Y.), 32, 35
St. Albans Golf Club (N.Y.), 130
St. Andrew's Golf Club (Yonkers, N.Y.), 33, 110, 114, 126–128, 138–142, 146–148, 173
St. Andrews (Scotland), 46, 95, 111, 138, 191–192, 204
Salem Witch Trials, 26
San Diego Open, 59, 60, 64–66
Sanders (family; see Gregory, Ann), 73
Sanderson, Julia, 168
Sands, Willie, 159–160
Sandy Mount Hole (Shinnecock Hills), 46
Sarazen, Gene, 9, 11–13, 18, 50, 130, 134, 180, 185, 195–199, *198*, 201
Sargent, Nan, 155–156
Saturday Night Fever (movie), 10
Senior Open Championship, 203
Schenectady Mallet (putter), 94–96, 98
Schneiter, George, 62
Scotch Hills Country Club (New Jersey), 48, 143–145
Scotland, 46, 93, 111, 113–114, 138, 142, 147, 179, 193–194
Secret Service, 22
Senior Championship, 203
Senior Tour, 87, 206
Sewall, Samuel, 26
Shady Rest Golf Club (New Jersey), 4, 143–145
Shinnecock Bay, 120
Shinnecock Hills Golf Club (Long Island, N.Y.), 43–44, 46, 119–120, 126, 128, 139–140, 142–143, 150, 153–155, 157–158, 160–162, 172–173
Shinnecock Indians, 43–45, 158

Shinnecock Indian Reservation, 44
Shippen, John, 43–48, *47,* 51, 67,
   84, 119–120, 144-145, 158
Shippen, Mrs. William, 155
Sifford, Charles, 51, 67, 81–87, *85*
Simmons College School of Social
   Work (Boston), 166
Simpson, John, 39–41
Singh, Vijay, 57
The Small Hole (Shinnecock
   Hills), 46
Smith, Alex, 168
Smith, Horton, 52, 59–60, 63–68,
   195–198, 205
Snead, Sam, 14, 16–17, 58, 61,
   69, 123, 181
Snow Golf, 3–4
Sorenstam, Annika, 156
Space Jam (animated movie), 175
Spaulding, A.G. & Bros., 103,
   188–189
Spaulding White Ball, 188–189
Spaulding Wizard Ball, 188–189
Speed, John Gilmer, 150
Spiller, Bill, 59–68, *64*
Spoon (club), 1, 91
Staten Island Links (New York), 29
Stephenson, Jan, 172
Stirling, Alexa, 117–171
Stranahan, Frank, 79–80
Strickland, Cliff, 50
Suffragettes, 164
Swing Aid, 107, *107*

Talking Ball, 108
Tallmadge, Henry, 114
Tam O'Shanter Club (Chicago),
   61, 75
Tam O'Shanter Open, 61
Tee (wooden), 88-91, *89,* 191
Tee Sleeve, 191
Texas Open, 52–53, 186
Thanksgiving, 27–28
Thirteen Colonies, 26

Thomas, Mrs. W.B., 155
Thompson, Bertha, 163
Thorpe, Jim, 67, 87
Tiffany, 2
Time Magazine, 167–168, 172
Tin Cup (movie), 15, 23, 130–131
Tolhurst, Desmond, 142
Tour (PGA), 9–10, 13–14, 16–18,
   22–23, 50, 53–55, 58–68, 82,
   85–86, 123, 134, 181–182, 196
Tournament Players Bureau
   (PGA), 62
Travis, Walter, 95, 132
Travolta, John, 10, 13
Trevino, Lee, 53, 55
Turnbull, John, 48
Turnesa, Joe, 53
Turnure, Arthur Mrs., 155

United Fund, 74
United Negro College Fund, 165
United Press, 72, 134, 202
Upham, John B., 147–148
Upper Course (*see* Baltusrol), 70
U.S. Amateur Open, 44, 95,
   120–121, 200
U.S. Patent Office, 89, 98
USGA (United States Golf
   Association), 1, 4, 18–19, 43, 45,
   50, 60–61, 64, 71, 74, 76,
   78–79, 81–82, 96, 100, 134,
   137, 153, 165, 181, 192, 194,
   200
U.S. Open, 9–13, 15–18, 21–23,
   43–47, 51, 70–72, 84, 132–135,
   140, 144–145, 160, 179–180,
   186–187, 191–192, 194–195,
   203–204
U.S. Public Links Championship,
   69
U.S. Steel, 73
U.S. Women's Amateur, 72,
   76–81, 117, 143, 153–172, 187,
   199–200

U.S. Women's Open, 136–137
Utica (New York), 68

Van Cortlandt Park (N.Y.), 32, 36,
    38, 102
Vardon, Harry, 132
Vardon, Tom, 132–133
Vare, Glenna Collett, 165, 199

Wake Forest University, 14–15
Wall Street Journal, 181
Washington, George, 125
Washington Golf Club (Georgia),
    124–125
Washington State Open, 54
Waterloo, 133
Watrous, Al, 9
Waverly Country Club (Portland,
    Ore.), 187
Webster, Charles, 38–39
Wells, Tom, 7–8
Wentworth Golf Club (England),
    199
Werden, Linc, 22, 137
West Farms Courthouse (New
    York), 38
Westchester-Biltmore Country
    Club (Rye, N.Y.), 170
Westchester County Golf Club,
    171, 185
Westfield Country Club (N.J.),
    143–144
Western Front, 179
Western Open, 9, 13, 53, 55, 58,
    200, 204
Wheeler, Howard "Cross Handed,"
    50, 67, 85
Whigham, H.G., 44

White Course (Shinnecock Hills),
    46, 143
White Dot Ball, 188
The White House, 22
Whitemarsh Valley Country Club
    (Philadelphia), 191–194
White, Stanford, 44
Whitney, Howard, 192
William of Orange, 26
Willis, Jr., William, 145
Willis, Sr., William, 144–145
Wilmington Country Club
    (Delaware), 165
Wilson-Western Sporting Goods,
    102–103, 199–201
Winchell, Walter, 60, 65
Winged Foot Golf Club
    (Mamaroneck, New York), 136
Winston, William, 177–178
Winter Tour, 56
Women's North and South
    Amateur Open, 170
Women's Sabbath Alliance, 31
Women's Texas Open, 200
Wood, Craig, 52, 58, 195
Woods, Tiger, 68, 167, 181, 184
World Championship, 14, 61
World Series, 130
World War One, 7, 102, 163, 166,
    203
World War Two, 14, 65, 165, 182
Wright, George, 202-203

X-Ray, 108

Yankee Stadium, 130
Yasuda, Kokichi, 56–57
"Yips," 123, 179, 184

About the Author

Peter F. Stevens is a journalist and an award-winning freelance writer. His many articles on overlooked but significant aspects of golf history are familiar to readers of *Golf Journal, Golf Magazine,* and many other publications. *The New York Times* has syndicated his golf pieces to newspapers nationwide. He has collaborated with PGA tour player and instructor Ted Kiegiel on the book *Balanced Golf* (Contemporary Books), has written articles about teaching professionals' innovative instructional techniques. He is a member of the Golf Writers of America. Stevens's other books are *The Mayflower Murderer and Other Forgotten Firsts in American History* (William Morrow; Quill), *Notorious and Notable New Englanders* (Down East), and *The Rogue's March: John Riley and the St. Patrick's Battalion, 1846–48* (Brassey's). He lives in Quincy, Massachusetts.